RASTAFARI

RESEARCH ASSOCIATES
SCHOOL TIMES PUBLICATIONS

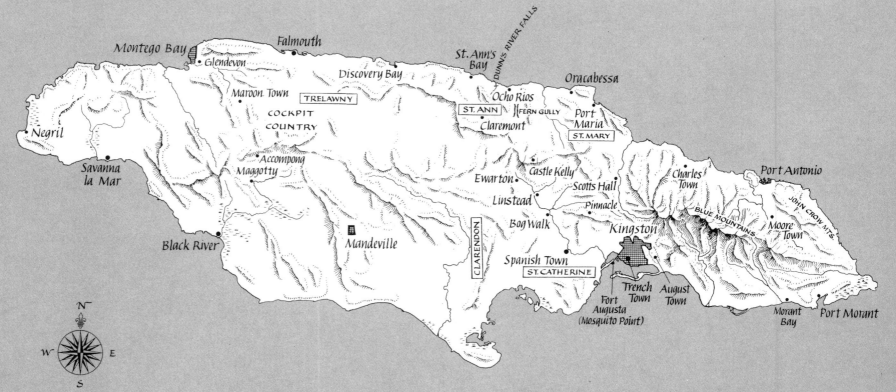

CARIBBEAN SEA

JAMAICA

Montego Bay
• Glendevon

Falmouth

Discovery Bay

DUNN'S RIVER FALLS

St. Ann's
Bay

Oracabessa

Maroon Town

TRELAWNY

Ocho Rios

ST. ANN

FERN GULLY

Port
Maria

COCKPIT
COUNTRY

Claremont

ST. MARY

Negril

Accompong
Maggotty

Ewarton

Castle Kelly

Scotts Hall

Charles
Town

Port Antonio

Savanna
la Mar

Linstead

Pinnacle

JOHN CROW MTS.

Bog Walk

BLUE MOUNTAINS

Moore
Town

Black River

Mandeville

CLARENDON

Kingston

Spanish Town

ST. CATHERINE

Fort
Augusta
(Mosquito Point)

Trench
Town

August
Town

Morant
Bay

Port Morant

N
W   E
S

CARIBBEAN SEA

0   Miles   20
0   Km   20

MAP BY PALACIOS

Distributed by
LUSHENA BOOKS
1804-06 West Irving Park Road
Chicago, IL 60613
TEL (773) 975-9945
FAX (773) 975-0045

RASTAFARI, A WAY OF LIFE

Published 1996, by
RESEARCH ASSOCIATES SCHOOL TIMES PUBLICATIONS
& FRONTLINE DISTRIBUTION INT'L , INC.
BY ARRANGEMENT WITH BANTAM / DOUBLEDAY DELL
COVER CONCEPT BY RAS SEKOU TAFARI
COVER DESIGN BY KASHIF MALIK HASSAN-EL
© 1979 TRACY NICHOLAS and BILL SPARROW
PREFACE COPYRIGHT © 1996 By SEKOU TAFARI

Library of Congress Card Catalog Number : 95-70815
ISBN : 0 94839 016 6

Published By
Research Associates School Times Publications
And
Frontline Distribution International, Inc.
751 East 75th Street
Chicago, IL 60619

CHICAGO · JAMAICA · LONDON · TRINIDAD, CARIBBEAN

CONTENTS

PREFACE TO THE RESEARCH ASSOCIATES EDITION

RASTAFARI: MY KING IS MY GOD AND MY GOD IS MY KING.

THE IMAGE OF GOD

"If the white man has the image of a white God, let him worship his God as he desires. If the yellow man's God is of his race let him worship his God as he sees fit. We as Negroes, have found a new ideal. Whilst our God has no color, yet it is human to see everything through your own spectacles, and since the white people have seen their God through white spectacles, we have only now started out (late though it may be) to see our God through our own spectacles. The God of Isaac and the God of Jacob let Him exist for the race that believes in the God of Isaac and the God of Jacob. We Negroes believe in the God of Ethiopia, the everlasting God - God the Father, God the Son and God the Holy Ghost, the One God of all ages. That is the God in whom we believe, but we shall worship Him through the spectacles of Ethiopia."

--- Marcus Garvey.

The Rastafari movement began in the Caribbean island of Jamaica during the late 1920's, out of the Pan-Africanist philosophy and ideology of Marcus Mosiah Garvey.

In 1914, Garvey and his first wife, Amy Ashwood, cofounded the Universal Negro Improvement Association (U.N.I.A.) and the African Community League (A.C.L.), in Jamaica before journeying to the United States of America, where he organized strong bases in various cities across the country.

The Honourable Marcus Mosiah Garvey advocated through the (U.N.I.A.), the need for self-reliance and interdependence by Africans in the diaspora. He asked, Where is the Blackman's army, his president, his government, his planes, and his ships? When the answer was in the negative he attempted to change the blackman's situation.

In 1925 Garvey was falsely arrested for mail fraud and later tried and convicted by the US government. He was imprisoned for two years in Atlanta. Whilst in Atlanta, he declared in one of his letters to his followers:

" If I die in Atlanta my work shall then only begin, but I shall live, in the physical or spiritual to see the day of Africa's glory. When I am dead wrap the mantle of the Red, Black and Green around me, for in the new life I shall rise with God's grace and blessing to lead the millions up the heights of triumph with the colors that you well know. Look for me in the whirlwind or the storm. Look for me all around you, for with God's grace, I shall come and bring with me countless millions of black slaves who have died in America and the West Indies, and the millions in Africa to aid you in the fight for Liberty, Freedom and Life."

In 1927, on returning to Jamaica after being deported from the U.S.A. Garvey was reported to have prophesied in one of his Sunday sermons:

"Look to Africa, where a Black King shall be crowned for the day of deliverance is near."

Therefore, when on November 2, 1930 Emperor Haile Selassie I was crowned in a gallant ceremony in Addis Ababa, Ethiopia, as King of Kings, Lord of Lords, Conquering Lion of the tribe of Judah, the masses of downpressed Africans in Jamaica were encouraged by their preachers and leaders to see His Imperial Majesty (HIM), who was the 225th Emperor from the lineage of King Solomon and Queen Makeda of Sheba to ascend the Ethiopian throne as their true Black living God reincarnate.

Today, some sixty-six years and more since its humble beginnings in the ghettoes and gullies of Jamaica, Rastafari as a way of life has manifested itself in every major part of the world in all walks of life. The colors Red, Gold and Green are now a symbol of identification for the movement in every Caribbean island, Britain, Europe, the U.S.A. and now it has returned to Africa - the motherland.

Rastafari is now on the move, manifesting itself in various progressive forms despite the negativity about the movement that is mostly espoused by those who are not very knowledgeable about this nation of people. There are so many distortions and misconceptions about Rastafari from within the mass media that we seem to be under attack in Babylon from both the barrel of the gun and the barrel of the pen.

Most people first awareness of Rasta came through listening to reggae music from its legends like the late Bob Marley, Peter Tosh, Garnet Silk and its current ambassadors such as Third World, Junior Reid, Culture, Bunny Wailer, Burning Spear, Jimmy Cliff, and the new sensational Capleton and many others who continue to proclaim His Majesty's name around the world in song and music.

Nonetheless, those who need to know will seek the path of knowledge in order to be adequately informed about this positive and upfull way of life, whose adherents not only smoke marijuana and play reggae music, but also work hard at all levels of society in all corners of the earth.

In 1996, the quest for knowledge on Rastafari is growing rapidly from various centres and institutions around the world, such as, penitentiaries, schools, libraries, and universities. Thus, the reintroduction and reissue of **Rastafari: A Way Of Life**, by Research Associates, written by Tracy Nicholas with exclusive photographs by Bill Sparrow, first published by Bantam Doubleday Dell in 1979, is a timely document that can fulfill the needs of those who are seeking more in depth information on Rastafari consciousness.

READ FOR KNOWLEDGE IS POWER.

Jah's Perfect Love,

Sekou Tafari,

Chicago, Illinois,

January 1996.

INTRODUCTION

You can see, hear, feel, smell, and even touch the West Indies in many places in the United States today. Whether they are blue-collar descendants of the Caribbean's former slave masters or Harlem cab drivers, the people of the West Indies have arrived in America. More and more the West Indian cadence—in speech, music, and all forms of culture—is being felt in America's urban centers, heard over America's airwaves. For the first time, Jamaica's reggae music is achieving a relatively potent stance in the popular-music industry. This grudging recognition is America's cold welcome: the giant nation proclaims itself but has difficulty practicing its avowed role as the world's melting pot. All races, colors, and religious persuasions can mingle in reality, but the dimension where our mentalities are shared is yet ahead of us. A pertinent witness to these things are manifested in the entertainment world, where minorities often earn their first chance to fly, is Ras Bob Marley, the spearhead of reggae. There have been other Jamaican music stars—Harry Belafonte, Jimmy Cliff, Peter Tosh, Toots and the Maytals, and Burning Spear, as well as those who play rock, ska, and dub music—but reggae is the sphere of Bob Marley, Rastafarian.

Rastafarians are seen now in the streets of Harlem and Philadelphia. They are in and around the many fast-growing West Indian communities in the United States. The newspapers give page-one reports of crimes committed by groups alleged to be Rastafarian. America, fascinated as always with the foreign, the unknown, grows curious about this "new" movement, which, once discovered, unfolds as old as time, as close as nature. Rastafari draws increasing attention. And remains a mystery.

The purpose here is to reflect some portions of Rastafarian reality as it is lived in Jamaica, West Indies. Not a definitive, structured study, *Rastafari* stands away from the clinical in an effort to transcend and communicate for the first time the fundamental philosophies and practices of this highly diverse and complex group.

Rastafari is, before it is anything else, a way of life. It offers approaches and answers to real problems black people face in daily living; it promotes spiritual resilience in the face of oppressive poverty and underdevelopment. It produces art, music, and cultural forms which can be universally recognized and appreciated. More important, Rastafari provides a positive self-image, an alternative, to people who need and cannot find or accept one elsewhere. Even with its black foundation and orientation, Rastafari is open to anyone, of any race, who chooses to discover and is able to accept it.

During my first visit to Jamaica, in the winter of 1970, I was returning to Oracabessa, on the island's North Shore, from Dunn's River Falls, a scenic tourist spot enjoyed even by vacationing Jamaicans. I noticed a tall black man with long twisted hair, walking his bicycle along the side of the road. His bearing was dignified even as his appearance bespoke extreme poverty. His eyes held anger, but focused somewhere beyond the immediate scene. I asked Mr. Smith, the driver, who that man was and was told, "Das a Rastaman, dey sum bad people. Criminal element, and very violent. Dey crazy, I tink, from puffin' dat ganja. An' ya nevah know now what dey gon ta do, so jus keep you safe and stay away, das all."

Contrary to Mr. Smith's advice, I did meet some Rastas on that visit—a wood carver and a painter—who impressed me as being some of the most peaceful people I'd ever known. I soon discovered that politics, economics, and world view played strong parts in the Rastafarian story, and on a later visit to Sangster's bookstore in Kingston I found further illumination. A pamphlet, by Rex Nettleford, M. G. Smith, and Roy Augier, sponsored by the University of the West Indies at Mona and published some ten years before, gave me some preliminary insights into the structure and meaning of Rastafarian lifestyle.

Since then I have visited Jamaica several times, meeting and talking with Rastafarians in all spheres of life throughout the island. I've met them in my native New York City, seen them in Boston and Washington, D.C. The information compiled for the text of this essay has germinated for quite some time and has been generated through a variety of experiences with Rastafarians. The most compelling and concentrated experiences occurred during a visit to Jamaica in the spring of 1976, when I spent my days among Rastas and was one of two (the second being photographer Bill Sparrow) non-Rastas to attend the annual grounation celebration in praise of Haile Selassie.

The Rastas are a most sensitive group about research. Recent revelations of CIA activity in Latin America and elsewhere have brought the Rastas' natural cautiousness to a fine point, and no one is above suspicion. When I entered a Rasta camp with writer's paraphernalia—pen, pad, tapes, mike, and recorder—to record my interviews and experiences among them, I found the tables turned —I was being questioned and taped. When the bredren were relatively satisfied that this book was an effort to reflect and not judge them, we could begin.

Being a woman in this context was no simple task—for complex reasons. On my first visit to a Temple of Rastafari I was greeted by a group of twenty bredren, who screamed, moaned, and shouted "Hellfire and damnation," "You have crossed Selassie I," "Condemned things," and "Shame in our house." I had only walked through the doorway. I listened, bewildered, as one Rasta recommended that they invoke "divine mercy" on this "daughter." I was told I sinned by entering the Temple bareheaded and by wearing pants. Like some gentle breeze, a woman appeared from nowhere, bringing me a scarf to cover my head. As I tied it on, she disappeared as quietly and swiftly as she had come. I sat down and did not speak until spoken to, when I think the bredren were surprised at my discussion of the concept of the book, its value, and my interest in doing it.

The depth and intensity of my "inquisition" in themselves were testaments to the nature of Rastafari. The Rastas have already achieved the indemnity of notoriety in their own culture, and that experience has taught them caution in communicating to the outside world. After two days of questioning, I was able to begin work, exhausted but pleased by the fact that we started from a position of knowing each other as people before we knew each other as functional parts of a publication.

In coming to know Rastafari, the first thing to be recognized is that it is not a cult, a religion, an ideology, a cultural revival, or a revolutionary political movement. Rastafari cannot be defined in these terms because it flows beyond, contradicting each of them and all of them. Religiously, it begins with the ancient and fundamental beliefs of Hebrew theocracy. Culturally, it has multiple facets, ranging from Africa to Jamaica with some Anglo-Hispanic accents. Socially, it is bound to some degree by the fabric of Jamaican life. Politically, it has interplayed with forces of the black freedom movement in rebellion against Jamaica's neocolonial reality. Economically, it is depressed, as is a majority of the Jamaican populace—and striving to clear the scars of that depression.

Rastafari: A Way of Life seeks to weave these elements into a common cloth, to be looked upon with comprehension by people of vastly different backgrounds, so that the sons and daughters of Rastafari may be perceived as a part of human reality and not as some deep, mysterious fear in a stranger's fantasy.

1. JAMAICAN EVOLUTION: AFRICAN AND EUROPEAN ORIGINS

Before Christopher Columbus sailed into Jamaica's Discovery Bay in 1494, the island was known as Xaymaca, the "isle of springs," by its native Arawak Indians. Within one hundred years of Columbus' staking the Spanish claim, the peaceful Arawak had been virtually exterminated: only seventy-four remained by the year 1511. Through the middle of the sixteenth century, the Spanish shared the island with nearly one thousand sailors of fortune and pirates of all nationalities. While African labor was imported to cultivate the land during this period, the Spaniards failed to develop any social system or cultural framework of substance. Therefore, in 1655, when Oliver Cromwell sent an English force to seize Jamaica as part of his planned offensive against Spanish possessions in the New World, he laid the groundwork upon which the sociopolitical and economic structures of the island would become thoroughly English.

During the first one hundred years of British rule, the population of the island increased drastically from 3,000 to 375,000—17,000 being Caucasian while the remainder were slaves imported from Africa. In this era, Jamaica underwent a transition. Initially a purveyor of tropical goods to England's North American colonies, Jamaica now began its existence as a "sugar island." While the British imported many slaves to Jamaica, they also exported great numbers from Jamaica to other Caribbean islands and North America. The slave trade and the sugar plantation became cemented as the foundation blocks of Jamaican economy.

Among the British planters in Jamaica, there was a high degree of absenteeism: most of them preferred to enjoy their financial prosperity in England and allowed lawyers to manage their sugar estates for them. This factor became crucial in the shaping of Jamaica's character as part of the New World. For the planters living in England, Jamaica was just the site of another sugar factory and, as such, was a purely economic entity. At times it was thought to be more profitable to work the slaves to death and replace them, rather than expend concern and money for their physical health. There was no crisis of conscience over slavery in Jamaica as there was at times on the other islands. The lack of social structure and concern for the slaves' well-being played a part in the island's long history of rebellion. According to Jamaican scholar Orlando Patterson:

Perhaps the most striking feature of the island during the

first ninety years of British rule is the fact that it can only with difficulty be described as a society . . . This was essentially a society of immigrants and transients . . . Unlike the slave systems of the American South or the majority of the Iberian colonies, there was here no ruling class who, infused with the pioneer spirit, were committed to the social well-being and cultural development of their community . . . The sociological consequence was a shambled patchwork of social relationships, which, in its excessive commitment to the sole goal of quick profits, discarded all aspects of the social institutions that are generally considered as the basic prerequisites of normal social life: marriage, the family, education, religion . . .[1]

The slaves who comprised the majority of Jamaica's population came primarily from the culturally diversified Gold Coast region of Africa. In later years, importation from the Gold Coast fluctuated, and slaves were brought in from Angola, the Congo, Dahomey, and Madagascar.

As time passed and various levels of communication and interaction developed between the masters and the slaves, certain folklore arose among the masters about slaves from different regions of Africa. Malagasy slaves died off too quickly; Angola slaves ran away from their masters or killed themselves—and believed, in dying, they were going home again. Ibos from Nigeria preferred suicide to servitude. On the whole, Gold Coast slaves were the favorites. In the eighteenth century almost half the slaves came from the Gold Coast. But by 1790 the Gold Coast was virtually a depleted source, and the importation of Angolans and Yorubas increased. The hundreds of thousands of slaves imported to Jamaica had very little in common, and yet a great deal in common.

Wrested from their tribal lands and linguistic groups and cast into a foreign hemisphere and a most oppressive way of life, their developing experience, either in survival or death, forged a common link among them. Their differing languages and dialects hindered communication among them but served as a positive force among the masters in preventing organized slave rebellions. The strongest common bond among the slaves quickly became apparent to the masters, though its importance was somewhat underestimated. This link lived in the commonality of religious philosophy and practices. Though the rites had differed somewhat from people to people in their African homelands, the basic religious functions and values derived from one fundamental philosophy. In Jamaica, even given the diversified origins of the slaves, the religious earmarks of voodoo predominated. In Angola and the Congo the Petro rite was practiced, while the Fons and Ewes from Dahomey and slaves from regions of the Gold Coast maintained the Arada rite. From Nigeria the Ibos and Yorubas used still another variation of voodoo. All forms of voodoo shared the features of the dance, the drums, the rhythm, and the spectrum of gods, or *loa,* through whom one falls under a trance or becomes possessed. The importance of this link is expressed in a statement by Janheinz Jahn in *Muntu:*

The religious dances were all the slaves had to remind them of their home . . . In their possession, surrendered to the old gods, for a short time they could feel themselves free once more. Where they could they came together to be near to Africa . . . the more the slave-owners suppressed and punished the dancers, the dearer, the more sacred did they become to the slaves . . . their religion became a secret cult, the faithful became sworn brothers, their secret meeting became the cell of resistance.[2]

While voodoo itself took root mainly in Haiti, where the greatest concentration of Dahomeans served bondage, in Jamaica *pocomania* (the little madness or possession) evolved out of a mixture of differing forms of voodoo brought from Africa. What common links survived were strong, as Jamaican slaves suffered one of the highest mortality rates of any of the islands. The growth in their population was achieved almost entirely by the importation of fresh Africans. Despite the survival of elements of their West African cultures, particularly religious elements, the shared ideas and values of the slaves rapidly collapsed under the oppression of slavery. The masters, as described by Patterson, held only profit making in common. The island of Jamaica was thus inhabited by two groups who had no shared traditions or experiences, who, by virtue of their roles on the island, hated and despised each other. It is in this context that Jamaica achieved the highest continuous level of rebellion of any Caribbean island. It is in this context that a "Maroon" pattern of resistance to slavery developed.

2. BLACK FREEDOM FIGHTERS: THE MAROONS AND MARCUS GARVEY

THE MAROONS

In 1655, when Cromwell ordered the invasion of Jamaica by English forces, a group of 1,500 Africans, whose Spanish masters fled the English invasion, escaped to the mountains. Known as the Maroons, they became notorious for their consistent harassment of and resistance to authorities while the English ruled Jamaica. The name "Maroon" derives from the Spanish *cimarrón,* meaning unruly, and, by extension, runaway.

Waging battle from the mountains with guerrilla tactics, the Maroons left the English at a loss both as to how to defend themselves and how to take the offensive. The main body of Maroons was headed by Juan de Bolas. Under his leadership they eventually surrendered to the English and won terms of pardon and freedom. A large number of Maroons, however, remained in the mountains, where they reproduced their numbers and were reinforced by fugitive slaves. Maroon settlements grew at Trelawny Town, Scott's Hall, Charles Town and Moore Town through the eighteenth century. A tremendous threat to the English, the Maroons not only attacked planters in the island's interior, but also gave African slaves a safe place to flee to. Their acts of rebellion and aggression against whites, including murder, intimidated the English and kept them from venturing inland from the seacoast.

In 1663 the lieutenant governor of the island issued a proclamation offering full, free pardon, twenty acres of land, and freedom from slavery to any Maroon who surrendered. Not one did. They were already free to do as they pleased—they had all the land they could use in the mountains and a moral obligation to themselves not to allow free and clear English dominion of the island. The Maroons continued to distress the English for more than forty years. During this time, more than forty-four Acts of Assembly were passed and at least £240,000 expended for suppression of the Maroons. By 1736, under the leadership of Cudjoe, the Maroons had grown so formidable that the British brought in two regiments of regular troops to fight them. By 1737 the British had launched an all-out campaign to conquer the Maroon forces. Fortresses and garrisons were built, packs of dogs obtained for tracking, and paid units of Mosquito Indians (imported from Central America), blacks, and mulattoes trained in bush fighting. The battling went on fiercely for months and was only ended when, on March 1, 1738, the British drew up a peace treaty and cosigned it with Cudjoe. The articles of pacification provided that the British cede some sixteen hundred acres of land to the Maroons and render set fees for the apprehension of fugitive slaves by the Maroons.

Little did the British suspect the coming of a second Maroon war more than fifty years later. This fierce conflict also culminated in a treaty, under the terms of which all Maroons were to surrender to the British by January 1, 1796. In addition, it was decided by an Act of Assembly that the most dangerous group of Maroons, the Trelawnys, should be banished forever from Jamaica. Subsequently, under orders of the Jamaican administration, the Trelawny Maroons were placed aboard a ship bound for Halifax, Nova Scotia. There, they lived in Preston, a settlement once inhabited by escaped American slaves who had since been repatriated to Sierra Leone, on the West Coast of Africa. Under the supervision of an official Jamaican emissary, the Trelawnys were employed to build a large fortress. Upon successful completion of the project, it was suggested that the Maroons remain in Nova Scotia as indentured servants. In reaction both to this suggestion and to the extremely harsh Nova Scotia winters, the Trelawnys made an official request to be removed to a warmer climate. While the Nova Scotian government had made concerted attempts to acculturate the Trelawnys to their new environment through intensive educational instruction in Christianity, it was the Maroons' absolute refusal to change their polygamous style of life that finally convinced the Nova Scotian government that their efforts were futile. By 1799 the Trelawnys were in open protest against remaining any longer in the bitter cold climate and refused to work. The upkeep of the idle protesters cost the Nova Scotian government £10,000 a year, which led the government to agree to try to send the Trelawnys to Sierra Leone, where the American slaves had gone before them. After prolonged negotiations, the government of Sierra Leone finally agreed to accept the Trelawnys. In 1800 the exiled Maroons sailed to Freetown, Sierra Leone.

To this day Jamaican Maroons continue to live in their mountain communities, particularly in the Cockpit Country of Trelawny Parish—a hilly, densely forested area, with limestone denudations which give the hills a "cockpit" effect. The Maroons are fiercely proud of having won a treaty from the British and have avoided most turnings toward modern civilization. In maintaining a world unto themselves, the Maroons are protecting their essentially unaltered African culture. Some change in this pattern seems to be developing through the efforts of the island's tourism agencies, so that today commercialized as well as real Maroons can be found in their mountain homes. The commercially oriented Maroon accepts Western culture enough to provide guided tours of Maroon Town, once Trelawny Town, in the Cockpit Country, to tourists, researchers, and the curious. The real Maroon disdains this means of livelihood, choosing insulation in basically African environs and having little contact with the Western world.

MARCUS GARVEY

A ghostlike chant lies over a heavy bass beat, drifting:

> No one remembers old Marcus Garvey,
> No one remembers old Marcus Garvey . . .
> No one remembers, no one.[1]

It is Burning Spear, a Jamaican reggae group, bringing back the ghost of Marcus Garvey in their album *Garvey's Ghost*. Burning Spear is singing its recognition of the man Marcus Garvey, who, more than any other single person, is the historical inspiration for the Rastas, reggae, a continuum of back-to-Africa movements, and the cultural revival Jamaica is experiencing today.

Born under the sign of Leo in the town of St. Ann's Bay, Jamaica, in 1887, Marcus Garvey was the youngest of eleven children in a poor family. He later wrote:

> As a child, I went to school with white boys and girls, like all other Negroes. We were not called Negroes then. I never heard the term Negro used once until I was about fourteen . . . It was then that I found for the first time that there was some difference in humanity, and that there were different races, each having its own separate and distinct social life. I did not care about the separation after I was told about it . . . I simply had no regrets.[2]

A descendant of the Maroons, Jamaica's first black freedom fighters, Garvey was said to be proud of his "pure black blood." Garvey's family was of the Jamaican "roots," and their economic struggles forced him to leave home at an early age to find work as a printer's appren-

tice in Kingston, thereby forfeiting a much hoped-for education. In Kingston, Garvey's perspective expanded rapidly, and in 1907, at the end of a major printers' strike in which he was involved, he determined to travel, see more of the world, and find out what the black man's reality was in other lands.

Starting out in Costa Rica, Garvey worked and traveled throughout the Caribbean and Latin America. As he came in contact with workers in many countries, he began developing his world view specifically on the problems of oppressed blacks, which was later to be heard by the entire world.

In 1912 Garvey traveled to London, where he reputedly enrolled in a college and came in contact with an Afro-Egyptian scholar, Duse Mohammed Ali, who awakened his interest in African culture and civilization. During this period, Garvey also read Booker T. Washington's *Up from Slavery,* which profoundly influenced him. When Garvey returned to Jamaica in 1914, he founded the Universal Negro Improvement and Conservation Association and African Communities League, whose objective was to establish educational and industrial colleges for Jamaican Negroes, on the model of Booker T. Washington's Tuskegee Institute in Alabama. The idea was accorded a positive response from the white power structure of Jamaica, indifference from the black masses, and hostile opposition from the mulatto class. Having obtained Booker T. Washington's promise of guidance and assistance, Garvey planned to visit the United States in 1915 to meet with him. The meeting never took place—Booker T. Washington died that year. In 1916 Garvey went to the United States, touring some thirty-eight states before choosing Harlem, in New York City, as his base of operations.

In 1917 Garvey established the Universal Negro Improvement Association, or UNIA, in Harlem. During the ten years of its existence, the UNIA claimed to have some two million black members. From this base, Garvey established an international weekly newspaper, *Negro World;* the Black Star Line, a shipping corporation founded for trading purposes and to transport blacks back to Africa; the Negro Factories Corporation; and countless subsidiary and related ventures.

Garvey's choice of time and place was a shrewd one. Harlem was not only the hub of black culture, the gathering ground of the Negro intelligentsia, literati, and artists, but also, and more importantly, the new home of thousands of black immigrants fresh from the South. The Ku Klux Klan, a secret southern organization formed shortly after the Civil War to suppress the newly acquired rights of blacks, was reborn in 1915 with "Americanism" as its objective. As the black influx to the northern "land of opportunity" grew, so too did "Jim Crowism," the discriminatory practices used by whites to prevent black equality, particularly in employment, transportation, and housing. Blacks necessarily became more militant, and a lesson was learned by all through the "Red Summer" race riots of 1919, when some 400,000 blacks returned from overseas service with the armed forces in World War I to find discrimination and its attendant frustrations awaiting them.

Marcus Garvey had arrived in the United States at the peak of the "Negro Renaissance." His doctrine of "Africa for the Africans" was solidly rebuffed by the black intelligentsia, most notably by the scholar W. E. B. Du Bois, who wrote in *Crisis* magazine that "Marcus Garvey is without doubt, the most dangerous enemy of the Negro race in America and the world . . . He is either a lunatic or a traitor." The predominantly light-skinned Negro intelligentsia could not relate to Garvey's call for Negro resettlement in Africa and was horrified by his interactions with the Ku Klux Klan, which naturally supported sending Negroes back to Africa and reserving America for whites only.

While the black intelligentsia opposed him, Garvey managed to step into a powerful role of leadership among the black masses, attracting a following which has never been equaled in the United States. Where the intellectual approach failed to move the black masses, Garvey spoke directly to their needs, frustrations, and hopes:

> The political re-adjustment of the world means this—that every race must find a home; hence the great cry of Palestine for the Jews—Ireland for the Irish—India for the Indians and simultaneously Negroes are raising the cry of "Africa for the Africans," those at home and those abroad.
>
> It is a cry for political re-adjustment along natural lines, and this re-adjustment has come out of the war of 1914–18, because we, as Negroes, realize that if we allow the world to adjust itself politically without taking thought for ourselves, we would be lost to the world in another few decades.[3]

Garvey's strength of leadership evolved from several forces which worked in combination with the conditions of black people in the United States and the Caribbean. Growing up a lower-class black in color-caste Jamaica, he experienced the concrete oppression of poverty. He also had an insatiable curiosity for knowledge about the black race, as well as a remarkable personal drive for power and domination. A fiery speaker in the evangelical style, Garvey was the first public figure to draw a connection between blacks in the West Indies, North and South America, and Africa. The fundamental elements of his philosophy were the self-redemption of the black race and the return of that race to the African continent to restore it to its ancient glory. Garvey drew upon biblical references constantly in his exhortations to blacks on the subjects of race purity, the chaos of the world, the spiritual brotherhood of man, the crime of injustice, the price of leadership, and the true solution of the Negro problem. In *The Philosophy and Opinions of Marcus Garvey,* his wife, Amy Jacques-Garvey, quotes his appeal to Africa:

> "Wake up Ethiopia! Wake up Africa! Let us work toward the one glorious end of a free, redeemed and mighty nation. Let Africa be a bright star among the constellation of nations." Garvey's advice to "all friendly whites" was, "Remember, give Africa a long berth, for one day God and His hosts shall bring Princes out of Egypt and Ethiopia shall stretch forth her hands."[4]

The crucial connection between Garvey and the Rastafarians arises from his prophecy, "Look to Africa, when a Black King shall be crowned, for the day of deliverance is near." This was accepted as a prophecy come true after Ras Tafari was crowned Emperor of Ethiopia in 1930, taking the name Haile Selassie. The Rastafarians acknowledge Garvey as a prophet and visionary, but they do not credit him with the initial inspiration for their philosophy and world view, despite his statements that suggest a strong influence:

> We Negroes believe in the God of Ethiopia, the everlasting God—God the Father, God the Son and God the Holy Ghost, the one God of all ages. That is the God in whom we believe, but we shall worship Him through the spectacles of Ethiopia.[5]

In the 1920s Marcus Garvey was able to organize and endow with power the largest Pan-African organization in history under the slogan, "One God, One Aim, One Destiny." His downfall, and the eventual disintegration of the UNIA and all its subsidiaries, came from Garvey's attempt to infuse his movement with personal, rather than organizational, power. He failed to surround himself with efficient, trustworthy people and failed as well to see that he couldn't lead and organize, too. Garvey would sell stocks without recording the sale, trusting to memory alone. In 1922, when he and three officers of the UNIA were arrested for mail fraud, the United States Government leaped on the tangle of UNIA finances, and Garvey's position became virtually indefensible. In 1923 Garvey was tried, found guilty, and sent to jail, but was released pending appeal. When his appeal was rejected, Garvey was incarcerated in the Atlanta Penitentiary. In a message to the UNIA from the Atlanta prison, Garvey strove to reassure his followers:

We have gradually won our way back into the confidence of the God of Africa, and He shall speak with the voice of thunder, that shall shake the pillars of a corrupt and unjust world, and once more restore Ethiopia to her ancient glory.[6]

In December 1927 President Calvin Coolidge commuted Garvey's sentence, allegedly in return for UNIA support given in the 1924 presidential election. Deported to Jamaica, Garvey began to organize again. He traveled throughout the West Indies and Central America, visiting various UNIA headquarters, attempting to shore up the broken pieces of his movement. When he voyaged to London in 1928 and spoke before a nearly empty Albert Hall, the signs of Garvey's fall from power were clear. He returned to Jamaica in an attempt to reorganize, but in 1935 he finally transferred headquarters to London, where he died in 1940. Garvey had once prophetically said, "Leadership means everything —pain, blood, death."[7]

In February of 1972 I held an interview with Amy Jacques-Garvey, widow of Marcus, at her memorabilia-filled home on Mona Road in Kingston. The interview ranged widely, the seventy-six-year-old Mrs. Garvey being an elucidating and captivating conversationalist. An extraordinarily courageous and dedicated woman, Mrs. Garvey was then still waging her husband's battle for the uplift of the black race. She told me, "Garvey never believed in hate, because it's poison. You can spend time hating and hating and hating, when you could spend time loving and loving and loving your own kind and building up unity." Amy Jacques-Garvey found her husband's rise to power in America to be both logical and triumphant, as she reflected, "White people have always given us hand-picked leaders. For instance, Du Bois—highly educated, protégé of white people, who dubbed him a leader. He never tried to rally the poor blacks. He taught at Fisk University but never rallied the sharecroppers and poor people there. He was a brilliant scholar, but not a leader of the black masses—and he never tried to be."

"Black people," she said, "want a revolution for change, like it took the Russians and Chinese years to achieve. You can have cadres of activists, but running out in the street with a gun is not revolution, it's damned silliness. You've got to have everybody organized, like soldiers, to do the right thing at the right time. This is how America will be brought to her feet, to recognize that black people have built their bridges, cities, nursed their babies . . ."

I asked Amy Jacques-Garvey what Marcus Garvey would do if he were still alive. She sighed. "Things have changed so much. Almost all of Africa is independent—they need technical skills, men with business acumen, etc. I think Marcus would try to establish this sort of reciprocity between African and Afro-American blacks."

Marcus Garvey's death in 1940 and Amy Jacques-Garvey's death in 1975 could never be seen as an end to their shared philosophies and opinions. Garvey's activism profoundly affected many blacks throughout the world. Pan-Africanism and black liberation movements during the past forty years have used Garveyism symbolically, in the red (blood), black (earth), and green (life, growth) colors he popularized, and ideologically in their programs as well. In fact, nearly every black movement in recent American history inherits some legacy from Marcus Garvey—through the Urban League, the Black Panthers, the Republic of New Africa, People United to Save Humanity (PUSH), the Nation of Islam, and other groups, Garvey's influence lives on. His memory certainly lives among the Rastafarians of his homeland. Whatever the historical analysis of social change in Jamaica, Marcus Garvey can be said to be at the root of it all. And yet Burning Spear sings, "No one remembers old Marcus Garvey . . . No one remembers, no one."

3. NEOCOLONIALISM: CLASS AND COLOR

Today, Jamaica's population is just over two million, of which one and three-quarter million are black, while the remainder is mixed between Creoles, whites, Chinese, and East Indians. On this seemingly paradisical island, with its searing sun, tropical climate, mountains, valleys, and swaying palm trees, 5 per cent of the population, predominantly the white establishment, owns 90 per cent of the wealth.

The dilemma of Jamaica's "roots," or masses, today arises from the island's neocolonial status. Once freed from British dominion, Jamaica became an uncharted economic entity, with the responsibilities, but not the means, for independence. Kwame Nkrumah, the late Ghanian leader, put it this way:

The essence of neo-colonialism is that the State which is subject to it is, in theory, independent and has all the outward trappings of international sovereignty. In reality its economic system and thus its political policy is directed from outside . . . Neo-colonialism is also the worst form of imperialism. For those who practise it, it means power without responsibility and for those who suffer from it, it means exploitation without redress.[1]

Some 50 per cent of Jamaica's population over the age of fifteen is plagued by illiteracy. The Jamaican government estimates that among people twelve to twenty-two years of age, 40 per cent are unemployed. Those who are employed work in menial and service positions, catering to the tourist trade and the upper classes, or working in the bauxite industry and on the sugar and banana plantations. Those Jamaicans who are educated tend more and more to leave the island, migrating to the United States, Great Britain, and Canada in search of the better life.

Dividing lines on the island are very clear—they are determined by class and color. Except under certain circumstances, in Jamaica black-skinned people comprise the lowest class. Brown-skinned people may subsist at a slightly higher level, while light-skinned people find their way to the middle and upper classes—the "good life"—with comparative ease. But nothing in Jamaica insures success so easily as being white—and the closer a person is, both in coloration and manner, to being white, the better is his or her chance for success. The European-supremacy ethic remains alive, perhaps not so much in the minds of Jamaicans themselves as in the socioeconomic structure of their reality. And this identity matrix alone is enough to keep the island in constant political turmoil.

The island's two major sources of livelihood—bauxite mining and the tourist trade—depend upon the cheap labor and service of the black masses. The downtrodden poor, the backbone of the economy, are not quite subservient cogs in the wheel. In Jamaica, the black masses generally dislike the mining and plantation executives, and the tourists, who can afford to live or vacation in luxury in paradisical environs while they, the "roots," remain poor, overworked, and uneducated. The ruling class and the tourists, in turn, look down on the black masses for their poverty and ignorance. It is the vicious circle of spiraling neocolonialism, and the average Jamaican is aware of the network of forces which interplay in controlling his or her life.

Between the rich and poor of Jamaica is a small buffering group—the coloreds/Creoles/mulattoes. Because of their lighter complexions, they have achieved higher education and consequently a more substantive level of income. Their relative success is a testament to the "liberal" nature of the white establishment. However, most Creoles covertly disdain the whites because they themselves are so close to, yet so far away from, the white race and the power that comes with it. The Creoles also look down upon the blacks because blacks are poor and helpless, yet related to them. The blacks in turn don't like the Creoles, who mistakenly think they are not black and are better for it. Outside of these patterns exists the East Indian or Chinese, for example, who is relegated to the buffering status of the Creoles, but is not accepted by them; nor do they accept the Creoles as their equals. The fact is, in Jamaica, if two people are different from one another, they're never seen as equals and can't be. Racial lines are a fact of life—everyone is aware of this and of what their status is, relative to their color.

Racial awareness seems to be a double-edged sword in Jamaica. While this awareness cuts what would logically be overwhelming racial tension in half, there is always an undercurrent, made real by problems of poverty and underdevelopment on the island, which reveals the need of the black roots to be set free, to be accorded equal opportunity. Periods of peace and quiet are necessarily, if not naturally, followed by periods of dissent and dissatisfaction. It is probably some form of miracle that Jamaica in recent years has not experienced the numerous *coups d'état* that have characterized similar nations' internal searches for equilibrium.

The miracle may walk in the human form of Michael Manley, Jamaica's fifty-three-year-old Prime Minister. Regarded by some as a visionary, Manley is a light-skinned man, ironically well-accepted by the Rastas and the black masses, as demonstrated by his 1976 re-election victory. From day to day, Michael Manley walks the tightrope between the state of economic solvency ("democratic socialism"), which he hopes to bring the island, and open mutiny by the middle class, who fear some of the means—particularly Cuban assistance and other third-world linkages—that might solve the inherent problems of Jamaica's neocolonialism.

Whatever may be the outcome of the shifting scales of power in Jamaica, the island remains the most politically dynamic and culturally diversified in the Caribbean. States of emergency and political dissent and unrest, while inconvenient and undesirable for the tourist trade, are signals of a struggling sovereignty's attempt to settle age-old disputes of race, class, and color and to develop a productive, expansive way of life which will be equitable for all its citizens.

4. RASTAFARIAN BEGINNINGS

Any Rasta will tell you that Rastafarian beginnings are not in Jamaica, but in Africa. All of Africa symbolizes a homeland, and a holy land, to the Rastafarians. Their roots are African.

The first Rastafarians appeared in Jamaica in 1930, at the time of Ras Tafari's coronation as Emperor of Ethiopia. Through the 1920s, Jamaica had experienced the prophetic activities of two native sons, Bedward and Garvey. Bedward, who eventually died confined in a mental hospital, founded several Jamaica Baptist churches on the island, the largest being in August Town, which is in eastern Kingston. Garvey built an international Pan-African movement with a larger black membership than had ever been seen. As described earlier, one of his prophecies went, "Look to Africa, when a Black King shall be crowned, for the day of deliverance is near." In 1930, when Ras Tafari was crowned Emperor Haile Selassie I, King of Kings, Lord of Lords, Conquering Lion of the Tribe of Judah, Garveyites and many Jamaicans looked to the Scriptures. There, in Revelation 5:2–5, they found:

And I saw a strong angel proclaiming with a loud voice, Who is worthy to open the book and to loose the seals thereof? And no man in heaven, nor in earth, neither under the earth, was able to open the book, nor to look thereon. And I wept much, because no man was found worthy to open and to read the book, neither to look thereon. And one of the elders saith unto me, Weep not: behold, the Lion of the tribe of Judah, the root of David, hath prevailed to open the book, and to loose the seven seals thereof.

Haile Selassie, who claimed to be a direct descendant of David, was 225th in a line of Ethiopian kings stretching in unbroken succession from the time of King Solomon and the Queen of Sheba. With hair like wool, like the Lamb. Haile Selassie excited those Jamaicans who awaited their Messiah.

The customarily religious and newly African-conscious Jamaican populace welcomed these events with some wonder. In the streets of Kingston, preachers on the corners began to voice their belief in the divinity of His Imperial Majesty Emperor Haile Selassie I. Among the early proponents of the Selassie-as-Messiah theory were Leonard P. Howell, J. N. Hibert, Archibald Dunkley, Robert Hinds, and Altamont Reed. As most street preachers do, they had established individual styles and approaches. But, try as they might to be unique, they found developing among them a common acceptance of

His Imperial Majesty as the Living God, the returned Messiah. A search of the Scriptures began, seeking anything and everything that might support their reverence of Haile Selassie. The following passages are among those interpreted as prosphesying the coming of a new King in the person of Haile Selassie I and the redemption of God's chosen people:

Ezekiel 37:19, 22–25: Say unto them, Thus saith the Lord God; Behold, I will take the stick of Joseph, which is in the hand of Ephraim, and the tribes of Israel his fellows, and will put them with him, even with the stick of Judah, and make them one stick, and they shall be one in mine hand . . . And I will make them one nation in the land upon the mountains of Israel; and one king shall be king to them all: and they shall be no more two nations, neither shall they be divided into two kingdoms any more at all: Neither shall they defile themselves any more with their idols, nor with their detestable things, nor with any of their transgressions: but I will save them out of all their dwelling-places, wherein they have sinned, and will cleanse them: so shall they be my people, and I will be their God. And David my servant shall be king over them; and they all shall have one shepherd: they shall also walk in my judgments, and observe my statutes, and do them. And they shall dwell in the land that I have given unto Jacob my servant, wherein your fathers have dwelt; and they shall dwell therein, even they, and their children, and their children's children for ever: and my servant David shall be their prince for ever.

Isaiah 43:1–15, 24–28, 65: 9: But now thus saith the Lord that created thee, O Jacob, and he that formed thee, O Israel, Fear not: for I have redeemed thee, I have called thee by thy name; thou art mine. When thou passest through the waters, I will be with thee; and through the rivers, they shall not overflow thee: when thou walkest through the fire, thou shalt not be burned; neither shall the flame kindle upon thee. For I am the Lord thy God, the Holy One of Israel, thy Saviour: I gave Egypt for thy ransom, Ethiopia and Seba for thee. Since thou wast precious in my sight, thou hast been honourable, and I have loved thee: therefore will I give men for thee, and people for thy life. Fear not for I am with thee: I will bring thy seed from the east and gather thee from the west; I will say to the north, Give up; and to the south, Keep not back: bring my sons from far, and my daughters from the ends of the earth; Even every one that is called by my name: for I have created him for my glory, I have formed him; yea I have made him. Bring forth the blind people that have eyes, and the deaf that have ears. Let all the nations be gathered together, and let the people be assembled: who among them can declare this, and shew us former things? let them bring forth their witnesses, that they may be justified: or let them hear, and say, It is truth. Ye are my witnesses, saith the Lord, and my servant whom I have chosen: that ye may know and believe me, and understand that I am he: before me there was no God formed, neither shall there be after me. I, even I, am the Lord; and beside me there is no saviour. I have declared, and have saved, and I have shewed, when there was no strange god among you: therefore ye are my witnesses, saith the Lord, that I am God. Yea, before the day was I am he; and there is none that can deliver out of my hand: I will work, and who shall let it? Thus saith the Lord, your redeemer, the Holy One of Israel; For your sake I have sent to Babylon, and have brought down all their nobles, and the Chaldeans, whose cry is in the ships. I am the Lord, your Holy One, the creator of Israel, your King . . . Thou hast brought me no sweet cane with money, neither hast thou filled me with the fat of thy sacrifices: but thou hast made me to serve with thy sins, thou hast wearied me with thine iniquities. I, even I, am he that blotteth out thy transgressions for mine own sake, and will not remember thy sins. Put me in remembrance: let us plead together: declare thou, that thou mayest be justified. Thy first father hath sinned, and thy teachers have transgressed against me. Therefore I have profaned the princes of the sanctuary, and have given Jacob to the curse, and Israel to reproaches. . . . And I will bring forth a seed out of Jacob, and out of Judah an inheritor of my mountains: and mine elect shall inherit it, and my servants shall dwell there.

Revelation 1:14, 17, 18: His head and his hairs were white like wool, as white as snow; and his eyes were as a flame of fire . . . And he laid his right hand upon me, saying unto me, Fear not; I am the first and the last: I am he that liveth, and was dead, and behold, I am alive for evermore, Amen; and have the keys of hell and death.

At the same time, another, more secular group was developing in Kingston. Led by Paul Ervington, Vernal Davis, and others, it shared Marcus Garvey's doctrines of social reform and migration to Africa. These men independently explored the teachings of Howell, Hibbert, and Dunkley, and in 1934 they too recognized Haile Selassie as the Living God.

In the meantime, Hibbert began to develop the Ethiopian Coptic Church, while Dunkley based his teachings on the King James version of the Bible. In an ensuing struggle for leadership of this now-large movement, Howell triumphed, using the best propaganda to generate the largest following. His movement spread from Kingston east to the town of Port Morant, where he was arrested in 1934 for selling more than five thousand photographs of Haile Selassie as passports to Ethiopia. Howell spent two years in prison, during which time Italy invaded Ethiopia, causing Haile Selassie's name to be spotlighted internationally. To the growing group of believers in Haile Selassie's divinity, Revelation 19:19 was fulfilled: "And I saw the beast, and the kings of the earth, and their armies, gathered together to make war against him that sat on the horse and against his army."

When, in 1936, Haile Selassie made an impassioned plea to the League of Nations against the Italian invasion of his empire, he was perceived by many in Jamaica to represent the Lamb: "And out of his mouth goeth a sharp sword, that with it he should smite the nations" (Revelation 19:15). And Revelation 19:20 was later fulfilled when the Emperor made his triumphant return to Ethiopia from exile in 1941: "And the beast was taken, and with him the false prophet that wrought miracles before him, with which he deceived them that had received the mark of the beast, and them that worship his image. These both were cast alive into a lake of fire burning with brimstone."

In 1935 the *Jamaica Times* published accounts of the activities of the Niyabingi Order of Warriors in Ethiopia. Reportedly led by His Imperial Majesty Haile Selassie I, the Niyabingi Order was to achieve the overthrow of white domination by racial war. In Jamaica, "Niyabingi" came to be defined as "death to all black and white oppressors." Some men locally known as "Ras Tafaris" came to be called "Niya men"; the idea of violence as a tool for freedom spread like wildfire, and in 1935 and 1936 all leaders associated with the movement were repeatedly arrested on suspicion of rebellion.

Upon his release from prison, Howell purchased an abandoned estate northwest of Kingston and in 1941 founded "Pinnacle," a Rastafarian community of sixteen hundred, on behalf of the Ethiopian Salvation Society. Under Howell's direction, the residents of Pinnacle grew two crops—yams for subsistence and ganja, or marijuana, which was illegal, for cash. Newspaper and Rastafarian reports said Howell represented himself as God and lived in the "big house" with thirteen or more common-law wives. Throughout 1941 the police raided Pinnacle regularly and arrested Rastafarians on charges of growing ganja and committing acts of violence. Howell, convicted on assault charges but not for growing ganja, spent two more years in prison. Upon his return to Pinnacle in 1943, he developed a corps of guardsmen who grew their hair long and were known as "locksmen" or "Ethiopian warriors." A clear doctrine of violence emerged, as Howell's warriors, disputing property claims, raided their unprotected neighbors. Over the next ten years, police surveillance grew in proportion to the spread of the Rastafarian movement, and conflict between the two became nearly a rule of thumb. In 1954 some 163 members of the Pinnacle community were arrested in a ganja "bust." Howell was tried and acquitted, but he returned this time to Kingston, scarred by rejection: his Pinnacle brethren refused to accept his claims of divinity. (The *Jamaica Daily Gleaner* of July 31, 1941, had quoted Howell speaking to a follower: "I will give you 96 lashes, I will beat you and let you know to pay no taxes. I am Haile Selassie, neither you nor the government have any lands here.") In 1960 Howell was confined to a mental hospital.

It is clear that the movement's developmental dynamics were complex, often prone to the demands and excesses of a single leader. However, it is also clear that the Jamaican origins of Rastafari appeared almost as spontaneous combustion in many different places at the same time. After the 1954 raid on Pinnacle, many more locksmen began to appear in Kingston, and other, loosely related groups also emerged. The movement was talking to the people, and they responded, increasing its membership steadily. The general establishment perspective on the Rastas was one of disgust and contempt, especially for locksmen. However, the Rastafarian movement has survived power struggles, leadership crises, repeated arrests and police harassment and has grown, changed, and today is a part of Jamaican reality.

5. THE RASTA WORLD VIEW

A primary objective of Rastafari is to revitalize African and natural styles and forms of life among black Jamaicans. John Hearne, a Jamaican scholar, writes in his essay in the pamphlet "Our Heritage" that the brown-skinned Jamaican under colonial rule "learned to doubt his own capacity for original thought or expression; learned, indeed, to view any native achievement with suspicion if not contempt. He learned to distrust his own judgment and to reserve opinion until the seal of approval had been given abroad."[1]

Black Jamaicans, educated and trained under British colonial auspices, learned that a key to survival was to carry a higher regard for things European than for things African. If anything, blacks were taught to despise and fear everything reminiscent of their African heritage. In imitating the "supreme" European ethics in every possible way, blacks negated their own identities, rendering dignity and self-esteem unreachable, impossible. Hearne warns that, "the fact that this imitation was servile, sometimes clumsy and often ridiculous should not blind us to the fact that it was also thorough. It might have been uncreative and in some measure stifling but it penetrated deeply into the consciousness of not only the brown middle class but the black peasantry and working class who are the majority of the island's inhabitants."[2]

Rastafari transposes Africa from the bottom to the top politically, aesthetically, and culturally. Rastas want black people to be their natural selves without fear, to have dignity, to know who they are and where they came from. Rastas would say that the forced transportation, or "smuggling," of millions of blacks from the continent of Africa to be slaves on the islands and mainlands of the New World provoked an imbalance that has not yet been set straight. The results of the direct use of techniques by slave traders and masters to disconnect the slaves from their social and cultural heritages are seen in the breakup of families, the destruction of shared rituals —the dance, the drums—the outlawing of traditional African religious ceremonies, and the separation from each other of slaves speaking the same language. These experiences, however long ago they occurred, have taken a severe toll of the health of the black psyche, and the Rastas advocate present usage of direct and specific techniques to reclaim a lost and marvelous heritage. These techniques permeate Rastafarian reality. Through their diet, dress, hair style, speech, language, and political and spiritual beliefs, most Rastas believe they are redressing a wrong, reversing a pattern, reclaiming the past.

The Rastas say that the black race lost its heritage through its own shortcomings. They recognize that Europeans imposed the power of the gun and the system of slavery upon blacks. But Europeans were only able to do so because blacks had strayed from the holy, divine way of living that was given them in the Bible, as God's chosen people. Almost from the beginning of time, they violated their holiness and happiness by worshiping more than one God, killing one another, stealing, lying. Whether or not blacks were informed by the Bible itself, Rastas say they (the blacks) knew the word of God. Nonetheless, blacks sinned against Creation, and their enslavement and life ever since is seen as a punishment by God, or Jah, as the Rastas know Him. For these reasons, they say, blacks are poor, uneducated, powerless, and oppressed—and will remain so until they rediscover and accept the divinity of Jah and their own potential to be "upright" human beings by living properly.

Black sinners in particular are obliged to save themselves, the Rastafarians say, because blacks are Jah's chosen people. Rastafarians say they have existed since the foundation of Creation:

"I'm from heaven. I'm from Zion the people call heaven. From the foundation of Creation, I was not just born, I was what Him talking to. I was smuggled from my father's waistline, emptied in the abcess of my mother's womb, and bursted forth upon this land as a mirror to reflect the divine qualities of Rastafari."

The Scriptures are fundamental to the Rasta world view. They do not look on the Bible as the "good book" —everything has good and evil in it. Over time, the Bible has been altered from its original state. For political and economic reasons, things have been edited out and different concepts and explanations patched in— especially by the translators for King James I of England. Therefore, the Rastas are particularly selective about what they believe from the Scriptures. Generally, they point to the books of Genesis, Exodus, Leviticus, Numbers, Deuteronomy, Psalms, Song of Solomon, Isaiah, Ezekiel, Timothy, Corinthians, Hebrews, and Revelation to demonstrate their philosophy.

In Genesis 1:26, after God/Jah has created the heaven and the earth, night and day, He says, "Let *us* make man in *our* image, after *our* likeness . . ." The Rastas say he was talking *to* someone—them—that they are the original, "sheeplike people," chosen by God/Jah. They cite Genesis 1:27—"So God created man in his *own* image, in the image of God created he him; male and female created he them"—to demonstrate that men and women were created equal. Then Jah blessed them and told them to "be fruitful, and multiply, and replenish the earth . . ." The Rastas say that clearly the black and colored peoples did replenish the earth—they are the majority. Then, later, Jah created Adam and Eve, man before woman this time, to till the ground. Adam and Eve are seen as the origin of the white race. Jah did not tell *them* to be fruitful and multiply, and so from the time that Adam and Eve had sex they were condemned. Jah himself is seen as black: "For the hurt of the daughter of my people I am hurt; I am black . . ." (Jeremiah 8:21). And in the Song of Songs, which is Solomon's: "I am black, but comely, O ye daughters of Jerusalem, as the tents of Kedar, as the curtains of Solomon. Look not upon me, because I am black, because the sun hath looked upon me. . . . His head is as the most fine gold, his locks are bushy, and black as a raven" (1:5–6; 5:11).

Once in contact with the white race, blacks compounded their sins by emulating the evil, unnatural ways of their oppressors. A Rastaman told me:

"It's just because black man do not realize who they are, and how powerful they are. Because black man is so easy to be bribed by other nation's qualities, they forget their principles."

The white world, Western civilization, is Babylon, a decadent, doomed, misguided, and corrupt society, in Rastafarian philosophy. Babylon is prevented from understanding, or achieving, the Rasta model of divine existence or correct living and, in fact, can only do evil. Rastafarians cite Revelation 17:1–5:

And there came one of the seven angels which had the seven vials, and talked with me, saying unto me, Come hither; I will show unto thee the judgment of the great whore that sitteth upon many waters: With whom the kings of the earth have committed fornication, and the inhabitants of the earth have been made drunk with the wine of her fornication. So he carried me away in the spirit into the wilderness: and I saw a woman sit upon a scarlet coloured beast, full of names of blasphemy, having seven heads and ten horns. And the woman was arrayed in purple and scarlet colour, and decked with gold and precious stones and pearls, having a golden cup in her

hand full of abominations and filthiness of her fornication: And upon her forehead was a name written, MYSTERY, BABYLON THE GREAT, THE MOTHER OF HARLOTS AND ABOMINATIONS OF THE EARTH.

Rastafarians see Babylon as a nation of intellectuals, explains Ras Hu-I, a force among Rastas in the Montego Bay area:

"Western man are guided by their intelligence, and that is where their intelligence reaches. They have no divine qualities, no divine inspiration. They go by selective concepts. They have no spiritual diagnosis. They go by *A, B, C*. They have no divine function. No divine principle. You have black man, too, like that, you know, who are the carbon copy of his slave master. Like a roast breadfruit. You seen a roast breadfruit? White on the inside, black on the outside."

Race is a strong issue for the Rastas, but is not the key issue. Rastas accept as fact that the white race, the oppressors, are in league with Satan and the Pope. The Pope is the head of Babylon and leads the oppression and mental enslavement of the black man. Nevertheless, it is thought to be possible for a white man to break the chains of his condemnation and follow a holy way of life, if his commitment and perservance are strong enough.

Beyond their belief that the black race is a chosen one which will rise again, the Rastas perceive many blacks to be lost sinners, as well as whites. However, the direction that life on earth is taking, as determined by the dominion of the Western powers—Babylon—is unnatural, undesirable, destructive. Rastas can see this, they say, in the epidemic spread of cancer (when the body's cells become "denatured"), the prevalence of environmental pollution, war, famine, crime, and violence. And the price to be paid for wrong living is a heavy one. Ras Hu-I explains:

"The Paris peace talks, SALT, all these things cannot bridge the gap between destruction and life. Not one shall stand. All of them shall be destroyed by their own hands. No one would like to dead. How is it the world don't try hard enough to find a solution? Western man feels it's impossible. It's not. But man don't try. All your intelligence cannot stop the lost and dreadful moment when you struggle, lifeless . . ."

"Life everliving," as the Rastas say, is their reward for following the holy ways prescribed in the Bible and will be their salvation as the rest of the world destroys itself. Living properly, naturally, and giving praise to Jah through every deed are the keys to living forever, in some form. The Rasta idea of heaven on earth is for right-living people to repatriate to Ethiopia, which is seen in two ways—as the geopolitical entity in East Africa and as the entire African continent, Æthiopia, as it was called by the Greeks in ancient times. Ethiopia in either sense is considered the cradle of civilization by the Rastas: Addis Ababa is thought to be Zion. Just as important, Ethiopia is the birthplace of His Imperial Majesty Haile Selassie I, whose coronation signified the redemption of black people. For the Jamaican Rasta, Haile Selassie is Ras Tafari, the son, or human manifestation, of Jah. The name "Haile Selassie" means "the in-strument and power of the Trinity," which some Rastas transpose into a natural framework—"the divine trinity of heat, air, and water." Rastas say it is natural for the Messiah to return as a King, through Haile Selassie, as Bongo Lenny explains:

"My father leave his radiant throne above and pass through the lineage of man, not as a common man, but as a royal man."

The Rastafarians see both good and evil in all—including their late Messiah Haile Selassie. In defense against criticisms of his centrist, monarchic rule over Ethiopia, the Rastas say that, like any ruler over men on earth, Selassie was prone to the complex contradictions that a royal man must face. Selassie, who was the world's oldest and longest-ruling monarch when deposed in 1974, began his reign in 1930 as a true reformer of the inequities of Ethiopian life. He increased the number of schools from 120 to 1,067 and the number of teachers twentyfold. He also abolished slavery. Haile Selassie, at the very least, represents the consummate imperial politician: while he brought progressive trends of modernization to Ethiopia, he was careful not to dislodge traditional societal patterns with the very tide he had created. As an Emperor, Haile Selassie was noted for his accessibility and openness, his ability to mix caution with flexibility in moving with the times. His consolidation of power in Ethiopia was gradual, well planned, and balanced, and this approach steered the nation clear of many stereotypical upheavals. His international statesmanship—by 1974 he was the most well-traveled head of state in the world—allowed Ethiopia to assume a position formerly held only by Western and industrialized nations.

In spite of his humanitarian efforts and tremendous skill in both internal and external politics, Haile Selassie ruled over a nation where 90 per cent of the population were poor, illiterate farmers without adequate food or medical care. On the eighteenth anniversary of his coronation, the Emperor said in an address in Addis Ababa:

> When we consider the time which is necessary to fulfill the needs of an individual it will easily be understood that the accomplishments of the needs of a vast country like Ethiopia can only be filled progressively and by stages. For the life of the world is such that periods of constructive achievement are followed by periods of destruction: the period of construction brings peace and the period of destruction brings uncertainty. We have always kept in mind that the union of the spiritual strength of the people with the material power of the independent nation provides the firm basis for our people to overcome the hardships and difficulties of life facing them in this world. Ethiopia relies on Almighty God and Natural Justice . . . imagination, devotion, perserverance, together with divine grace, will assure your success.[3]

The Rastafarians see Haile Selassie as a productive monarch who, despite his divinity, was limited by his human form and role in life. Citing Hebrews 2:9–10, they note, as a parallel, the fact that Christ was held to human limitations:

> But we see Jesus, who was made a little lower than the angels for the suffering of death, crowned with glory and honour; that he by the grace of God should taste death for every man. For it became him, for whom are all things, and by whom are all things, in bringing many sons unto glory, to make the captain of their salvation perfect through sufferings.

Most Rastas do not deny or defend critiques of their most holy Ras Tafari, Haile Selassie I. They emphasize the positive, understand and do not dwell on the negative. The Emperor himself was not a Rastafarian, although he did know of the Rastas' existence and held an audience with their representatives when a Jamaican commission visited Ethiopia in 1960. He himself visited Jamaica in 1966, where he was thunderously received at the airport by thousands of Rastas attired in the finely intricate and colorful African cloth called "kinte," and long, flowing white robes. They waved palm fronds, Ethiopian flags and bunting, shot off firecrackers and rockets, played the drums, danced, chanted, and praised their Deliverer. Haile Selassie was the first African head of state to visit the island, and Rastafarians came from "the fastnesses of Wareika Hills [in Kingston], the wappen-bappens of Western Kingston, Accompong, Moore Town in John Crow Mountains, and every village from Negril to Morant Bay," traveling in "trucks, carts, hired buses, bikes, cars and drays," the *Daily Gleaner* reported.[4] The Emperor was visibly moved, shedding tears. The momentous event had been planned with great care —the government had even declared the day a public holiday. But, because of the crowd's enthusiasm, many of the airport ceremonies never took place: people were not presented, the red carpet was ignored, anthems were not played, and the biggest traffic jam in Kingston's history later blocked the parade route. At the airport, hundreds of Rastafarians crashed the receiving line of ministers and opposition leaders and wandered about under and around Haile Selassie's plane, not caring about the still-moving propellers. Finally, Mortimer Planno, a Rasta leader from Kingston, was called to address the crowd and calm them. This finally took effect, enabling the Emperor to leave the airport. The *Gleaner* reported that "long after the last car in the procession had left, the Rastas lingered on. They touched the wings of the plane and they smiled. They expressed their satisfaction. Then in small groups they drifted from the runway, leaving behind a pile of slippers and sandals, flagpoles, palm fronds, flags and a fatigued airport staff."[5]

The Rasta focus on Haile Selassie can be easily understood if one studies a speech he made in 1964 in California, which contributes to the Rastafarian world-view. Entitled "What Life Has Taught Me on the Question of Racial Discrimination," the address states:

That until the philosophy which holds one race superior and another inferior is finally and permanently discredited and abandoned; that until there are no longer first- and second-class citizens of any nation; that until the color of a man's skin is of no more significance than the color of his eyes; that until the basic human rights are guaranteed to all without regard to race; that until that day the dream of everlasting peace and world citizenship and the rule of international morality will remain in but a fleeting illusion to be pursued but never attained; and until the ignoble and unhappy regimes that hold our brothers in Angola, in Mozambique and in South Africa in subhuman bondage have been toppled and destroyed; until bigotry and prejudice and malicious and inhuman self-interest have been replaced by understanding and tolerance and goodwill; until all Africans stand and speak as free human beings, equal in the eyes of the Almighty; until that day, the African continent shall not know peace. We Africans will fight, if necessary, and we know that we shall win, as we are confident in the victory of good over evil.[6]

According to Rasta belief, the spirit of Rastafari is universal and eternal—Haile Selassie's death in 1975 has not diminished their faith in his divinity. The words of his California speech reappear on Bob Marley's album *Rastaman Vibration*. Sung over the heavy-bassed reggae beat, the song "War," with lyrics taken from the Emperor's speech, is a declaration, a demand, for freedom. Freedom, if anything, is the key issue for Rastas.

In Jamaica today Rastas' freedom is restricted by institutions they don't believe in. The police—agents of Babylon, of the establishment—represent a government which functions without the guidance of Jah and which therefore has no divine purpose. In the Rasta view, Jamaica is hell. Rastas will tell you that several hundred years ago it was a lovely island, but it has since been corrupted and defiled by man—notably by Babylon—and is now an outpost of oppression for the black man. Rastas say that deliverance will come only through right living and repatriation to Ethiopia. Most Rastas in Jamaica avoid working in traditional lower-class jobs —instead of picking bananas or stripping sugar cane, they co-operatively open auto repair shops or carve wooden art, play music, act, dance, farm, or teach. Rastas demand respect everywhere—"work is good, but slavery isn't"—and they don't like to be obligated to Babylon for their livelihoods.

Freedom, in Rastafarian philosophy, can be achieved through a twofold process. The first, a recognition of Babylon as an abominable way of life, condemned to destruction by hellfire and brimstone, is a rejection cycle: reject slavery, white supremacy, black inferiority, worldly possessions—reject everything Babylon has taught. The second—to be able to love yourself and others, know yourself and others, live in peace with yourself and others—is an acceptance cycle. According to Rasta philosophy, the acceptance cycle means accepting Rastafari, accepting yourself, and achieving the determination that peace and love will be the primary factors in your life. Jah, in his infinite grace, will respond to your divine qualities by protecting you and providing for your every need. Love, Unity, Peace, Equality, and Justice become both the common laws and the highest values of existence. And you become life everliving.

These are the fundamental aspects of the Rasta worldview. Rastafarians see themselves as the true Hebrews, black Hebrews—chosen by Jah, redeemed by Ras Tafari, the Living God, who was His Imperial Majesty Haile Selassie I of Ethiopia. They are a large, extended family of brethren, sons, sisters, and daughters, who will live on in peace and love long after Babylon has fallen.

In being free, each has the right to choose his or her own way; some Rastas accept this world-view, others accept parts of it. Orthodox followers of the Rasta faith grow dreadlocks as symbol of their devotion and holiness —others do not. Some Rastas say Jah is the Father, Ras Tafari is the Son, right-living Rastas are saints, and day-to-day Rastas are simply "bredren." Others say Ras Tafari is the Father and they are his sons and daughters. All Rastas, however, are seeking freedom, and their personal choices are made on that basis. But as Matthew 20:16 puts it, "Many be called, but few chosen." Ras Hu-I reasons thus:

"It takes time for a tree to shed its leaves and put on fresh ones. The tree reaches maturity, it sheds the leaf. If him is Rasta, him won't drop everything at one time unless him is dead. But as time goes on, him tread in higher qualities. That's how it go. From the foundation of Creation you have Rasta, you have follower of Rasta. Rasta is the son and daughter of Ras Tafari Selassie I. Heat, air, and water —the Trinity. Time is the Sun, Nature is the Moon, the stars are the children of Sun and Moon. The bright star is high (I), the fading ones are the people who have no glory, no divine glory. My father, Ras Tafari Selassie I is the Almighty . . . In every dispensation that the Almighty come on Creation, him set monuments to which no man can pass or can climb or can achieve. No one. Monuments: Noah, the ship; Moses, the Red Sea; Joshua, Samson, Elijah, right down to Christ. These men are men of examples. Christ—they can't kill him. They can't dead.

"Rasta is not something that just a person look upon, Rasta is sent to do a job. You see, Rastafari is a reality. Each and every man have Ras Tafari in them, therefore have divinity in them. They fail to nourish it and cherish it. They let the torrents of lust and evil overcome this part of divinity. One would have to have his own divine qualities as calling of the Almighty projected upon him. Divine quality is not a thing a person can adopt. Him just can't adopt it. By the action, thoughts, and deeds, you will know if it's divine qualities or just an adoption. It's hard

—you may find a congregation, and you have just only one divine person in there, and all of them claims to be Rasta. But the Rasta that have been selected from the foundation of Creation have been sent to live a life and to show the people who the Almighty really is."

6.   RASTA TALK 'BOUT I AND I

If you really want to know how Rastas think, listen to them talk. In addition to the Jamaican *patois* of the roots, which is less understandable to American ears than the accent of the British-schooled middle and upper classes, the Rastas have a language and vocabulary that is their own.

As if they lived in the days of the Wise Men, Rastas use words like "dispensation," "fullness," "hellfire," and "brimstone." The Rastas found these words in the Bible and have incorporated them into their vocabularies and their lives. Communication through speech, through words, bears moral and spiritual responsibility—Rastas don't play games with words. They say that in moral unity man's action is glorified and has a real effect, interacting with all human and other life forces. Therefore, meaning what you say wastes no human energy forces. It's divine economy, with morality.

Rastas make up words and transpose them, but they don't play games. Wordsound is power, as the Scriptures tell in describing the Lamb, or Ras Tafari, in Revelation 19:12, 13, 15:

> His eyes were as a flame of fire, and on his head were many crowns; and he had a name written, that no man knew, but he himself. And he was clothed with a vesture dipped in blood: and his name is called The Word of God . . . And out of his mouth goeth a sharp sword, that with it he should smite the nations: and he shall rule them with a rod of iron: and he treadeth the winepress of the fierceness and wrath of Almighty God.

"Wordsound is power." In Genesis, Jah created life, the heavens, and the earth simply by saying so, by speaking words. According to one Rasta, "By speaking, Rasta recreates the universe, striving for compassion, humility, love, and harmony."

For the Rastafarians, the most powerful and significant letter of the alphabet is also a word and a number: "I." I is part of His Imperial Majesty's title—Haile Selassie I. It is the last letter in Rastafar*i*. "I" is so important that a Rasta will never say "I went home," but would say instead "I and I went home," to include the presence and divinity of the Almighty with himself every time he speaks. "I and I" also includes bredren, who also say "I and I." In this simple way, through language, Rastafari is a community of people all the time. According to one Rasta:

> "I and I just utter words, and it manifests. All that I and I do is to project a life that is higher than the Christians'.

For Christian life, Christianity, is a profiteering organization. When Billy Graham, the CIA, on pulpit, the preaching of the gospel is over. I and I just project a life, and who want to follow it, follow it. Man see it and say, the life that that man living, each and every one shall live that life. Him say, 'I want to be a Rasta,' and him start to follow after I. It's just the life that they seen, showing the true pathway to life everliving. If I and I stumble or fall, slip or slide, him slide too."

"I and I," then, reminds the Rastafarian of his own obligation to live right and at the same time, it praises the Almighty. "I" is also used in combination with other words, to glorify them: by substituting "I" for a syllable, the Rastas create their own meanings. The word "power" becomes "I-ower," "thunder" "I-under," "total" "I-tal," and so on. The word "irie" (pronounced *eye-ree*), is an ultimate positive. "All is irie" means nothing could be better; the "irie heights" or "ites," in Rasta talk, are tantamount to heaven or a strongly uplifting spiritual feeling.

Rastas never say "Good morning." The morning is always good—it is man that is bad—and good. Likewise, a Rasta won't say "I and I will come back soon," but rather "I and I will come forward soon." "Back" and "return" are negative, nonprogressive words. So even if you mean "backward," you'll say "forward" and be understood. "Understood" is another word the Rastas change. Understanding, or comprehension, they say, is a transcedence, an uplifting—so why say *under*stood"? It's only logical to say *over*stood." In the same manner, "last" always becomes "first."

To "overstand" a conversation among Rasta sisters or bredren, you must first adjust to the fact that you're not hearing a "conversation." Any lengthy talking among Rastas is known as "reasoning." By using their thoughts and expressive capacities collectively, through Rastafari, Rastas feel they are sharing their experiences fully. It's a group doing. Not *from* one *to* another. Rastas reason *together,* they don't converse back and forth. It is what they call "spiritual diagnosis," as opposed to Babylon's "selective concepts," which, they feel, are linear, unnatural, and unproductive. Reasoning can be experienced on any topic—politics, sports, reggae or "dub" music, life, Rasta. Whatever the subject, reasoning is meant to be a putting together of minds. If you are not ready, willing, or able to put your mind together with Rastas and do some "deep" reasoning, then they will feel you are not ready to talk with them at all. Which you might not be.

People following the Rasta way of life greet one another by saying "Peace and love," "Peace, Rasta," "Love, Rasta." "Praises due Selassie I," or "Irie," in various combinations, and leave one another the same way. Depending upon the person, his age, and his style, he will be called, for example Ras Lenny, Rasta Lenny, or Bongo (black) Lenny. One Rastaman, called Iya Glenn, says that "iya" means "I live." Smiling, he chants: "A climb in the rung of the ladder. Just the chant of 'Iya Glenn' is the inspiration to take me higher."

Anywhere Rastas are, you'll hear them saying "seen" to one another, heads and dreads nodding in agreement. 'Seen" is a Rasta's way of saying "I know" or "I read you." It means that the words spoken, as if confirmed in physical reality, have been *seen*—totally comprehended and accepted. "Seen" also takes in the spiritual aspect of perception: a Rasta's view should be wide and open enough to take in things which are known, but not visible. "Seen" completes reality, adding vision to the process of communication.

Rastas who are angry or upset with someone will intone "Ras clot," "bongo clot," or "bumba clot," all of which are curses. Being called a "clot" is being told that you came as a blood clot, and not an ovum, from your mother's womb. Even the base curse, for Rasta, has the most natural of origins.

Perhaps nothing about Rasta talk—the words, the transpositions, the expressions—is as important as the *way* of Rasta talk. Many are natural poets, and every sentence, every thought, is expressed with rhythm, depth, and gestures that emphasize, in sound and measure, the meaning. In the temples of the Almighty Ras Tafari Selassie I, the bredren, sisters, and daughters chant their praises to Jah, and the chanting rises so powerfully, so harmonically that once over, it seems to linger through any silence, beyond any dusk or dawn. Rastas bring great drama to their speech as they intone passages from the Bible so vividly that Jamaica's lush foliage transforms, ever so subtly, to an Edenlike environment.

Which is what Rasta wants—to feel the power and strength of the natal connection to *Creation*—which allows Rasta to be perceived, by himself and others, as worthy, as holy. Speaking in biblical language almost transports Rasta back beyond his history of enslavement and oppression, to a time when his dignity was natural and not acquired or striven for. Through their word-sounds, Rastas create their power.

It is ironic that the Rastas have probably never read the works of anthropologists describing Nommo, the African "power of the word." In Jamaica, the Rastas conceptualize speech as a holy tool, which is certainly how it is viewed, and used, in a variety of African cultures. The many manifestations of Nommo/wordsound-is-power among Rastas bear witness to the fact that their goal—to go *forward* to Africa—is being realized in day-to-day living. And it happens as the Rastas would like it to, naturally. They know, fundamentally, without experiencing Africa, that their concept of language is natural and right. That it happens to carry over from centuries of African tradition is no accident. Rasta simply knows, without knowing, as things are "seen" without being seen.

7.   DIVINE THEOCRATIC GOVERNMENT

Rastafarians have only recently begun to develop themselves as an organized force across the island of Jamaica. Approximately three years ago, the Divine Theocratic Government of Rastafari Selassie I was founded by leaders of the movement representing Jamaica's Rasta population. The government at present is headed by a High Council of about fifteen men, whose daily activities range from teaching at the University of the West Indies to painting, to auto mechanics, medicine, art, and engineering. The High Council meets periodically to discuss the progress and problems of the movement and its members, to plan economic development, the annual "grounation" (a celebration honoring Rastafari Selassie I) and all manner of Rasta activity.

In the spring of 1976 the High Council concluded an unprecedented series of conferences with Jamaican Prime Minister Michael Manley. The conferences, termed successful by members of the High Council, took place in Kingston and centered on the theme of recognition of the Rastafarian movement as a legitimate and constructive force on the island and attempted to fulfill some of the Rastafarians' express economic and social needs. While it is improbable that any direct and immediate results will be evident, it is certain that the Rastas received a serious hearing from Manley, who was quoted in the New York *Times Magazine* of July 25, 1976, as saying that "Man has a deep need for a religious conviction, and Rasta resolves the contradiction of a white man's god in a colonial society . . . I think that the only Jamaican who truly knows who he is has to be the Rasta man." Social unrest in Jamaica will undoubtedly prevent Manley from handling Rasta concerns as liberally as he might. He must not further alienate the Jamaican establishment, which already fears his "socialist" leanings, transactions with Cuba, and economic approaches which may tend toward nationalization of some of the island's major industries and thus threaten the financial future of the managerial and upper classes.

The Divine Theocratic Government in Jamaica today is, quite naturally prone to the setbacks and operational difficulties of any emerging organization. While, to the outsider, the Divine Theocratic Government may seem relatively free of conflict, there are certainly internal struggles taking place which are catalysed by the rapid growth rate and the emerging, recognized political prowess of the Rastafarian movement as a whole. Despite Rastafarian attempts at and occasional successes in achieving unity of purpose and direction, there are conflicts of interest which arise primarily between leaders from Kingston and those from some of the island's rural areas. Because the Divine Theocratic Government has not yet developed a fully centralized structure, these clashes are usually not apparent, with individual Rasta leaders maintaining harmony over their respective domains. It is when the leaders come together that conflicts must be settled, through hours of discussion and debate, even displays of emotion, shouting, and screaming. However, for the most part the Divine Theocratic Government appears surprisingly cohesive for a fledgling organization. At this early stage in the existence of the Divine Theocratic Government, it is logical that these kinds of conflicts—sometimes more interpersonal than organizational—have to work themselves out. At some point, when the Divine Theocratic Government has developed beyond its Jamaican infancy, resolution of more serious conflicts will foretell the future of Rastafari as an organized force in Jamaica.

The basic quest of Rasta is the maintenance, among all people, of divine principles of life. All of these principles—honesty, loyalty, fear and love of God, self-attainment—are laid down in the Bible and are not meant to be added to, diminished, or otherwise altered by man. Man should only manifest. Man stays in tune with divine principles and qualities because of the manner of life he adopts—or, he loses touch with divine qualities for the same reason. A man who lusts, steals, lies, or otherwise defiles himself, his blackness, his holiness, is doomed to the perdition of life on earth without holiness or happiness. The man who lives by divine principles, who recognizes and upholds his divine qualities through all the actions he takes as he moves through life, develops an obligation to happiness and freedom. He must have both, and, by right, they must claim him.

One High Council member describes the Divine Theocratic Government like this:

"Theocratic Government is a divine government that shall rule Creation in Love, Purity, Holiness, and Unity with all the ingredients of Affection, Compassion, and Humility. The Theocratic Government was projected from the foundation of Creation. But because Lucifer polluted it, it broke apart. We come to reunite it into one gigantic force, that it must cover the whole world, like a water cover the sea. That's what the Theocratic Government are: we are no pain, no sickness, no tears, no woe, no man that eat dead cow and woman having birth control and man that put on panther [condom]. Because Satan and his host have been trampled under brutal feet of death. When we conquer Babylon, when we conquer the deceiver Pope under brutal feet of death, then it shall be one ruling government—theocracy. Combined with Time, Nature, and Space—those are the three ruling forces of theocracy. The Rainbow is the emblem, the dominion, and the power and the glory for all the Theocratic Government. That is his flag, the Rainbow. It's a government, a Divine Theocratic Government, and that's the reason why all who belongs to this Theocratic Government should project qualities. Not only talk it, but utilize it among others. Be a mirror, reflect qualities."

Another High Council member explains:

"The structure of the government is Selassie I. The column, main column, is Love, Purity, and Holiness. Divine qualities are combined to make up a structure. You may not find in each these qualities—but they have it in Rasta. They are within Rasta. But there are certain things that divine Rasta go by. Outside of that, you'll know that he's my bredren. I don't condemn my bredren. What they have done, I rebuke them over it, and edify them, but I don't condemn them."

The origin of theories of theocratic government is not easy to come across; very few secular analyses of theocracy exist. Theocracy is the system of laws for life that are recorded in the Bible as commanded to the Israelites by God, whom the Israelites accepted as their creator, the almighty being in their universe. The Rastafarians consider themselves to be the only true Israelites, descended from the tribe of Judah, although in their lexicon, God is called Jah. From the Rasta perspective, the Israelites—a group, a family, a nation of people—were in need of direction in order to survive the physical effects of raw greed, wars, hunger, and sickness that reigned over the lives of men in biblical days. They were also in need of spiritual guidance to help them cope with times of unfathomable natural cataclysms—earthquakes, floods, tornadoes. Jah, who created all these things, including man, was the only Being trustworthy to the task. And so they placed their trust in His ability to protect them and asked His trust in return, through developing patterns of chanting, prayer, and ritual celebration of His Holiness and their faith and love in Him.

Jah fulfilled the Israelites' needs by dictating, through Moses, commandments as to how to live and how not to live, where to live and where not to live. In return for their compliance with His demands, Jah promised to live among them, supplying their every need by virtue of His holy presence. As long as man followed the covenants commanded by Jah, man would encounter no sickness, hunger, or sorrow. In a treatise on Hebrew theocratic government, written in 1848, Dr. J. Cogswell stated,

> The worship of the true God was made the fundamental law of the Hebrew Theocracy. The Hebrews, when they attained quiet possession of the promised land and obeyed the laws of the Theocracy, enjoyed more freedom, [and] were better protected than any nation then on earth.[1]

The Rastafarians require worship of Jah, not only through participation in ritual and chanting ceremonies, but also through the daily action of life and thought a man or woman follows. In the Bible it is made clear that the punishments visited upon men and women for disobeying theocratic law would be as terrible as the rewards for their obedience would be marvelous. Divine power, in Rasta thought, is the power to do good and to reward, as well as the power to do evil and to punish. Jah is seen as the total Almighty Being, capable of performing both helpful and harmful acts. Rastafari is seen as attuned humanity, capable of augmenting or detracting from divine powers. All humanity is born with divine qualities, Rastas believe, but these qualities should be recognized, nurtured, and protected, holistically from childhood, in order for humanity to reach a spiritual and free apex.

In the Book of Exodus, Jah dictates to Moses the elementary principles of what the Rastas espouse today as Divine Theocratic Government. The moral covenants delivered to the people of Israel had their bases in the fabric of life as it was then lived on earth. A return to this mode of government would be in accord with the Rastafarian philosophy of following the fundamental laws of nature, with which they remain in tune. The Rastafarians may be one of the few groups on earth in the twentieth century who can realistically relate to natural law as given in the King James version of the Bible. Their way of life is very similar to that for which God's laws were prescribed through Moses. They can and do survive in the hills and countryside of Jamaica—they can and do survive in nature. It is one of their basic beliefs that natural survival is the only healthy and correct way of existence. Only to a limited extent do the Rastafarians need or desire to share in the "so-called advances" delivered by a Westernized, technologically dominated society.

What all black people need, according to Rastafari, can be found in the theocratic laws. In Exodus the Ten Commandments set a fundamental pattern of behavior, but the Israelites' Lord God continues to define rules for living through much of the Old Testament. While the Rastas are not inclined to follow specifications for worship and sacrifice—these are considered to be Westernized infusions into the basic meaning of the Bible, they are inclined to the following:

EXODUS

21:12—He that smiteth a man, so that he die, shall surely be put to death.

21:15—And he that smiteth his father, or his mother, shall surely be put to death.

21:16—And he that stealeth a man, and selleth him, or if he be found in his hand, he shall surely be put to death.

21:22—If men strive, and hurt a woman with child, so that her fruit depart from her, and yet no mischief follow: he shall be surely punished, according as the woman's husband will lay upon him; and he shall pay as the judges determine.

22:16—And if a man entice a maid that is not betrothed, and lie with her, he shall surely endow her to be his wife.

22:19—Whosoever lieth with a beast shall surely be put to death.

22:31—And ye shall be holy men unto me: neither shall ye eat any flesh that is torn of beasts in the field; ye shall cast it to the dogs.

LEVITICUS

11:41—And every creeping thing that creepeth upon the earth shall be an abomination; it shall not be eaten.

11:42—Whatsoever goeth upon the belly, and whatsoever goeth upon all four, or whatsoever hath more feet among all creeping things that creep upon the earth, them ye shall not eat; for they are an abomination.

11:44—For I am the LORD your God: ye shall therefore sanctify yourselves, and ye shall be holy; for I am holy: neither shall ye defile yourselves with any manner of creeping thing that creepeth upon the earth.

19:26—Ye shall not eat any thing with the blood; neither shall ye use enchantment, nor observe times.

19:27—Ye shall not round the corners of your heads, neither shalt thou mar the corners of thy beard.

19:28—Ye shall not make any cuttings in your flesh for the dead, nor print any marks upon you: I am the LORD.

The Divine Theocratic Government Rastafari Selassie I, in a mimeographed circular, demands of the members of its family and temple thus:

Thou shalt not take more than one woman or daughter unto yourself—anyone have two is full of lust. Any woman or daughter who has a man and found lying in bed with another Brethren are guilty of death—Our Father Rastafari has one Blessed Queen Omega. Brethren must not down-gress or brutalize their daughter or woman, do not cause her embarrassment in the congregation of brethren. She must not enter in the congregation unless her dress cover her knees. The daughter or woman that show her legs in the congregation must be put out of the audience of brethren because she is selling flesh for popularity and contributes to the society of lust.

Thou shalt not lie in bed with a put away daughter or woman. It is ungodly for a daughter to leave one brethren and a next brethren living with her in bed as wife and husband. A daughter and her Kingman who cannot live in peace, they should bring the differences in the Upper Room of Brethren from the Theocratic Temple. There the Brethren hear the confusion, and if there is no compassion offered to the Accused, they should live apart as widow and widower until Selassie I call us home.

Brethren should not infiltrate Ulterior Motives into the mind of daughters. The woman and daughters should not be romantic in the Presence of the Almighty, but should like unto Queen Omega. Daughters should not eat their Holy Chalice in the congregation.

Thou shalt not carry the three unclean spirits in the Holy Theocracy Temple of Our Creator Selassie I, they are condemned. Which are combs, scissors, and razors with a seal of death where no belly killer, birth controller, night vampire, sodomite thief, beggar, and drunkard. They will not enter in the Rest of Rastafari. He who do these corrupted and condemned things and defend these wickedness is wiped out of the book of life everliving and lost to communication with the Almighty, and walk in his own lust and corrupted desire.

Thou shalt not gamble or buy horse race, lottery, no bingo, no card-pack, dominoes, checkers, no liar thief and sluggers like spirit. WOE be unto the leader that drink rum, beer, or find himself in bar without reasons, or whore houses, cinemas, dance halls, parties or keep clubhouses or bars to entertain whoredom.

No brethren shall speak to his other brethren without the full dignity and majesty of love. One should not carry grievance against his brethren because he uses undignified sound, is not wise, and he who use these words are uncultured and have no tolerance. Rastafari help I and I to live these precedents.

Zion and her holy trumpets they blow away all missiles, bullets and misfortunes from Rasta. We fly under the tree of Life which beareth twelve different kind of fruit. I and I stand behind the Holy Altar of the Theocracy Temple of Rastafari Selassie I, we commend ourselves to Rastafari Holy Purity that no man's hands must capture I and I in prison. We must not be lit nor shot nor stabbed nor assailed or injured or wounded by anyone. Whoever keep these precedents is invisible. Anyone belong to this Theocracy Temple of Selassie, such person can't drown in any water nor burn in any fire, and no unjust verdict will ever be rendered against him.

To this hour, help I and I Father Rastafari the one only creator: I looked away to Oracles of Divinity and view across the threshold of life, I saw three men not yet very old. The first was Rastafari the Creator. The other was Rastafari the Almighty Infinite Selassie I. The third was Selassie I the Holiest Temple of Heaven and Earth. They protect my life and soul and blood, that I and my brethren must not fall in the abyss of the Earth. That stones, knives and spears may never cut I and I, that never a thief may steal the least from I. Whosoever is stronger and mightier than these three men, he may bitter assault if he cannot, or forever keep his peace with I and I.

The Rastafarians continue to develop the precepts of Divine Theocratic Government and to apply them to their own lives in Jamaica. They do not follow Divine Theocratic Government in opposition to the ruling People's National Party of Jamaica, but rather see the PNP, Jamaican government, constitution, and bureaucracy as mere temporal instruments of Babylon, created to obstruct natural living, to empower evil, and to oppress the holy. Some Rastafarians see and declare themselves, in words and actions, as warriors against that oppression, while others feel that peaceful living through theocracy will accomplish the long-term victory of good over evil.

Some Rastas worship regularly in the Temples of Rastafari established throughout the island. Others mix their religion with worship in the Ethiopian Orthodox Church, which is established also in the Sudan, Israel (Jerusalem), the United States (New York), and the West Indies. One of the earliest Christian Churches, the Ethiopian Orthodox has a large following in Jamaica, where its advocacy of blacks—Ethiopians—as the founders of civilization and Christianity develops self-respect and dignity among the black masses. The Ethiopian Orthodox Church's literature describes the Hamitic family—Ethiopians, Egyptians, Canaanites, and Chaldeans—as the fountainhead of civilization, which later spread throughout Africa, the Middle East, and the Orient. The Ethiopian Orthodox Church cites the fact that ancient historical books of India make reference to civilization arriving there from Ethiopia; that old Cushite kings were worshiped in India; that circumcision was introduced to Egypt from Ethiopia; that the Egyptian Pharaoh Khufu, an Ethiopian, was the builder of the Great Pyramid at Giza.

The spiritual and historical reference points of the Ethiopian Orthodox Church are not vastly dissimilar from those of Rastafarian philosophy, although the Church did not worship Haile Selassie, but accepted him as a God-serving Christian. However, the respective socioeconomic realities of the Church and Rastafari bring them into dynamic opposition, with the Church viewing the Rastas as a heathen, criminal element in Jamaica and the Rastas viewing the Church as an instrument of Babylon's oppression. Young Jamaicans who are raised in the Ethiopian Orthodox Church and become disillusioned often turn to Rastafari for relief, for a new way.

Rastafari supplies that new way, through the oldest way of life—divine theocracy. It says it's all right for young folks to smoke ganja, to dance and celebrate—it teaches them to eat ital (i.e., total, or natural) food for their own health and to love Rastafari for their own honor. Rastafari supports a positive image of Jamaican youth as black, even as the youths' parents often denigrate Africanness, preferring European culture and social dictates in the neocolonial style.

When the Rastas say that "love, purity and holiness

shall cover over the earth like a water cover the sea," they are noting the turning of a tide toward Rastafari. Spiritually and religiously, the gap between Rastafari and the Ethiopian Orthodox Church is not very great. For a populace raised in the Ethiopian Orthodox Church, the turn to Rasta is not a drastic one, but a possible turn to new religious freedoms and to comfort. Which is what a Rasta says he is—a comfort.

8. GANJA, THE MYSTIC HERB

"YOU MUST NEVER GANG JAH, FOR HE WILL KILL YOU," the Rastas say. "Ganja (pronounced "gonn'-jah") is the Jamaican name for marijuana, or *Cannabis indica*. The Rastas play on the wordsound, but most can be heard calling it "ganja" interchangeably with the more acceptable word from the Bible, "herb."

The history of ganja in Jamaica is almost as old as that of the island itself. The herb, which is now illegal to use, possess, or sell, may have been native to the island and used by the original Arawak inhabitants. It may have been imported from Africa or India. According to Lambros Comitas, coauthor with Vera Rubin, of *Ganja in Jamaica,* marijuana is not indigenous to the New World—it originated in Asia and "was gradually diffused through trade routes from Asia until it reached Europe . . . Eventually it was carried to the New World by Spanish Conquistadors about 1545 . . ."

Jamaica's tropical climate has been hospitable to the Indian strain of marijuana, as well as that said to come from Africa. "Ganja" is the East Indian name for herb, and, among Rastas, its highest form is called "kali," after the Indian goddess in whose honor ganja is smoked along the river Ganges.

Ganja is, perhaps, the strongest shared experience among Rastas. As individuals, they smoke it in "spliffs," comparable in construction to American "joints." The spliff is much larger, is cone-shaped, and is rolled with brown-bag paper, newspaper, or lining paper from cigarette packs. Four Rastas smoking spliffs will smoke four spliffs—one for each, no passing. The ceremonial *chillum* pipe, used for shared smoking, is a right-angle construction of bamboo, with a burning coal at its top which keeps the ganja lit. The pipe is passed among bredren, the smoke billowing until faces are no longer visible.

Ganja is the catalyst for many a long reasoning, stretching from the heat of the day into twilight. The smoking of ganja among Rastas is inspirational and has an opening effect. Rastas tend to become more jovial, relaxed, and visionary. They begin to share thoughts and meanings beyond the daily actions of life—or to look more fully into those daily actions. Rastas are also thinking so much and so often about the conditions of the world, especially the plight and direction of the black and oppressed, that ganja helps them relax with their heavy thoughts, instead of feeling strained or anxious because of them.

Rasta women do smoke ganja, but it may not be evident. Generally, they won't be found sitting around with a group of bredren smoking, but they might be on the sidelines somewhere pulling on a spliff. Nobody says that women shouldn't indulge in ganja, but there's an unspoken, agreed-upon opinion that women of propriety don't smoke in public. The attitude seems directed more toward the physical act of smoking than toward the smoking of ganja, for the illuminating qualities of the herb are considered beneficial to anyone's divine inspiration. Ganja makes it a little bit easier to reach the "irie ites," where the mellow feelings are.

But Rastas don't assume that everyone has the capacity to smoke cannabis—particularly ganja, a potent strain. Divine illumination is what everyone should be looking for, but not everyone is ready for it. Bredren will tell you of visitors who have passed out after one pull on the pipe. Regular smokers among the Rastas consume huge quantities of ganja daily. A Rasta's acquisition of ganja for a group of bredren may be the most important mission of the day. Unless something unusual happens, Rastas who smoke won't be without it.

Ras Hu-I will tell you of the black herb from the valley of Gojam in Ethiopia, so powerful that only the stupid or ignorant would smoke it—wise Rastas use it only in tea. Bongo Sylly, the wicka worker (wickerworker) advises that "all people don't know how to use herb correctly—if you don't," he warns, "use the tea." Sylly thinks some people are frightened by herb, and cannot control themselves with it. But, for him, it yields the desirable results of relaxing him, making him feel more calm and comfortable, more fluid and productive.

Sylly says: "Rastas grow herb for themselves. What's left gets taken and marketed in the trade, which give Rasta a bad name. Makes ganja a political herb, which it is not. It is a divine herb."

The distinction Sylly makes is a crucial one for Rastas. Any political or financial reference to herb, they feel, is a perversion of its real role and use value. The Rasta divine-use theory comes direct from the Bible—Genesis 1:11–12:

> And God said, Let the earth bring forth grass, the herb yielding seed, and the fruit tree yielding fruit after his kind, whose seed is in itself, upon the earth: and it was so. And the earth brought forth grass, and herb yielding seed after his kind . . . and God saw that it was good.

Ganja, then, is important to spiritual, mental, and physical health. Hu-I has found herb to have as many as thirteen different medicinal properties.

The divine sanction of herb in the Bible, according to Rastas, makes outlaws of governments who would forbid and suppress its use. It is thought that Babylon is afraid ganja will lead people to see the truth that living Babylon-way is a rotten way, an unholy way, to live. Certainly, the history of Rastas and ganja is one of repeated arrests for possession and usage since the Rastafarian movement began in the 1930s. Ganja smoking is widespread among the roots of Jamaica, but is frowned upon by the upper class which correlates ganja with crime, violence, laziness and a wanton, lower-class lifestyle. Ganja is the herb of the masses in Jamaica, but they have little political or economic influence to alter its legal status—the government currently penalizes the use, possession, and dealing of ganja. The development of ganja legislation in Jamaica is covered in depth by the authors of *Ganja in Jamaica*, but it can be noted here that the illegality of the herb in Jamaica is in no way related to its status in the United States, where it is ofttimes classified as a catalyst toward heroin and other hard-drug use. Jamaica has no heroin problem, and it is rare to find any drugs other than ganja in use or for sale there.

Rastas are not fearful or reticent about using ganja, despite its illegality. Their general attitude is that they're not doing anything wrong, and if they're relatively discreet, they won't get caught by Babylon. There are many political reasons unrelated to ganja which make the busting of Rastas for possession and use of it proportionately more frequent than it should be. Bongo Sylly remarks, "They no trouble me so much for use herb, but I must *hide* the herb from them to show respect for their authority."

9. DREADLOCK RASTA

An overt, identifying signal, dreadlocks are probably the most misunderstood aspect of the Rastafarian lifestyle. People regarding the long locks have all kinds of ideas as to how they get that way, and what they mean. It is all ironic to the Rasta because, for Rasta, nothing is more simple or natural than dreadlocks. Wearing dreadlocks, they feel, is just a part of good living.

In several of the Scriptures, the holy man is instructed not to alter his hair:

Leviticus 19:27—Ye shall not round the corners of your heads, neither shalt thou mar the corners of thy beard.

Leviticus 21:5—They shall not make baldness upon their head, neither shall they shave off the corner of their beard, nor make any cuttings in their flesh.

Numbers 6:5 (pertaining to those vowing to follow the ways of God)—All the days of the vow of his separation there shall no razor come upon his head: until the days be fulfilled, in the which he separateth himself unto the LORD, he shall be holy, and shall let the locks of the hair of his head grow.

On the foundation of these biblical commandments, the Rastas grow their long, unaltered locks as symbols of blackness, dignity, and honor. The longer the dreadlocks, the longer has been a Rasta's devotion to holy ways of living. The name "dreadlocks" signifies unholy peoples' fear of the dreadful power of the holy. It is appropriate, when you realize that the establishment in Jamaica often *does* dread the black man or woman wearing locks. Tourists and visitors to the island see black people wearing dreadlocks and envision violence, cannibalism, machetes flailing wildly against "civilization." Some Jamaicans, too, are made extremely uncomfortable by blacks wearing dreadlocks, who are an affirmation of the very blackness, the very Africanness, that their colonial upbringing has taught them to hide and deny—a facile rule of survival in a European-supremacy system. Others are simply afraid because they don't know the meaning of the locks and perceive wearing them simply as an aberration, a difference, a breaking of convention. But the wearing of dreadlocks means more. It is a testimonial among Rastas, signifying that, regardless of the dictates, fads, and reactions of style or society, the Rasta will choose to wear his hair as a holy man does—unaltered from its natural state, at all times.

Another truth about dreadlocks is that they're an indisputable racial characteristic. Formed simply by washing the hair and allowing it to dry without combing, brushing, or treating it in any way, real dreadlocks can only be grown by black people, whose quality of hair naturally entwines it into the long locks. Caucasian or Oriental hair does not grow into dreadlocks, although very curly hair may make an approximation. Dreadlocks are not braids, plaits, twists, or anything stylized. Rastas joke about "bathroom locks," worn by folks who can't really give up the comb but who do want the hip, "antisocial" effect of dreads and attempt to style their hair that way in the privacy of their bathrooms.

Ras Hu-I explains that dreadlocks are a quality of black, or sheeplike, people:

"To grow dreadlocks, just wash it and leave it, that's all. Because black people are already sheep. They have wool upon their head, while white people have hair. But black people prostitute themselves—they liken to a white man—for crown and title, gold and silver, and become goat by using comb, scissors, and razor. Those are the three revolutionary forces that Babylon and Pope have over the world. Which is politics, religion, and commerce—those are the only three sins upon creation. No other sin. Every sin that's committed upon this earth falls under those three elements. Every sin upon Creation. Comb, scissors, and razor. We know that. Rasta dreadlock wool is not something that has been prepared: man is born with it. Divine quality is not something that you can adopt. It was embedded in you from the foundation of creation—not something that can be prepared or manufactured . . . As a man destroys his hair, he destroys himself, his divine energy. Him will na produce nothing."

Hu-I adds that dreadlocks are "high-tension wires," which transmit divine energy and inspiration from Jah, the creator, to Rasta, the mirror. A Rasta without dreads is a "baldhead"—he cannot be taken seriously, because he does not display his commitment to the faith—and besides, how can anyone get a message to him? A Rasta without dreads is like a New York executive without a telephone—in dubious standing. On the other side of "high-tension wire" many people wear dreads for the style and don't attach any spiritual significance to them.

Dreadlocks, more than any other Rasta symbol, have serious political significance. Most dreadlock Rastas will take the precaution, before going from their homes out into the world, of pulling on a woolen tam, often in the African liberation colors of red, black, green, and gold. In this manner, Rastas are showing some respect for the authority of Babylon, whose agents are quick to tune in to the "criminal potential" of a locksman. And when a Rasta is arrested or taken in for questioning by the police, the first thing that is likely to happen to him is that his dreadlocks will be shorn. Rastas are infuriated by this practice, which they describe as wanton police brutality. In the Rasta view, as we have seen, dreadlocks are a function of spiritual belief and not simply a style of protest to be tampered with by agents of Babylon. A victim of police brutality will wear the scar—short hair—for a long time. Apparently, in the never-ending feud between the Rastas and the police, the cutting of dreadlocks has become something of a police sport. Clearly, it's not sport to the Rastaman, whose pride and identity—his dreadlocks—have been a long time growing.

Dreadlocks growing from the scalp and the beard are

totally natural. The hair grows much longer, much faster in locks. Visitors to Jamaica speculate that the Rastas cake their hair with red mud and have other unclean hair habits. However, the reddish tinge sometimes seen on the outer locks is not mud-induced, but comes from the exposure of the hair to the intense Jamaican sun—the hair bleaches naturally, taking on a reddish color.

For a Rastafarian initiate, growing dreadlocks is a primary sign of commitment to the faith. You must show your ability to contradict the social modes and customs of Babylon in the interest of Rastafari and your own divine qualities. Once you've begun to develop your "high-tension wires," all realms of life can open and be revealed to you through Rastafari.

10. ITAL FOOD

One Rasta says:

"Man should not eat mechanically: he should eat what grows from the soil. Agridishes. No dead flesh of any living thing that creepeth on the earth. All living things that grow from the earth."

"Agridishes," or foods which grow from the earth, are ital—total or natural—foods. They are not contaminated or denatured by any processing, additions, or deletions. Ras Hu-I, being a doctor, a healer, is fundamentally concerned with what the body takes in, as well as what functions it must perform to process healthfully what it does take in: eliminating that which is unneeded and that which has given everything it has to offer. The human body is seen as one of the miracles of Creation, of nature—it is a reflection of divinity, made in the image of Jah, and should be treated as such. Rastas believe that everything a man or woman does becomes a part of what he or she is. When Jah created the first people, he specified that all herbs bearing seed and trees bearing fruit would be as meat to them. The orthodox Rasta follows this dictate and refuses to soil and desecrate his or her system by consuming inferior beings or dead flesh: only life can give life. "He shall not make his stomach a cemetery," says the Rasta. Consuming meat, fish, eggs, or poultry makes your stomach "a cemetery," as you are taking in dead flesh. It is logical, through theocratic thought, for a living mechanism of nature, the human body, to only take in living things. In the Rasta view, canned foods are also dead—and "buried."

Some Rastas won't use silverware or plates. Their food is eaten from coconut bowls with their fingers or with utensils shaped from coconut shells or wood. Rastas can and do identify this practice with their African roots—on the Aethiopian continent more fingers are used to eat, then washed and used again, than forks or any other utensils.

Rastas don't like to drink the processed water that's delivered through the Jamaican water supply system—and many of them live in areas yet to be fully supplied with running water. Particularly in the rural and exurban areas, Rastas collect rain water in barrels and use it for drinking and for preparing and cooking food. Bathing and the washing of garments are often done in streams or ponds.

The preparation of ital food is an art shared by bredren and sisters alike—no sexual role models or stereotypes apply here. One of the staple dishes is rice and peas. Popular throughout the West Indies, its flavor is usually enchanced with pork, beef, or goat meat. Since Rastas don't eat dead flesh or use it in any connection with ital food, they first go through a time-consuming process of grating coconut to produce a flavorful milk in which natural rice is cooked. Then vegetables are added —peas, red beans, onions, tomatoes, country peppers. All go into the same large, steaming iron pot of rice which sits over a fire. It may be contradictory to cook in metal pots and refuse metal utensils for eating—but it seems the Rastas feel that there is no point in wasting a lot of coconut bowls by attempting to cook in them.

The fruits and vegetables indigenous to Jamaica comprise a major portion of the ital diet. Papayas, coconuts, oranges, bananas, breadfruit, ginger nuts, watermelons, plantains, star apples, mangoes, pineapples, ackees, chochos, and calalus are all eaten, some in their natural state, some cooked or stewed according to special Rasta recipes. The Rastas even have a way to peel oranges so that all the juice and fruit can be swallowed without a drop or morsel being lost.

It is believed that, by following the ital diet, people can insure their own long lives and health. Ras Hu-I contends that using the ital diet is a major protection against cancer, which, he explains, occurs when cells become "denatured" through the intake of or exposure to unnatural or antinatural elements. He pauses, silent, and then mysteriously states that he knows the cure for cancer. That's all. But, he says, "There is today a greater menace to civilization than that of war. The name of this menace is malnutrition. We eat too much, and most of what we eat is poison to our system—'half of what we eat keeps us alive, the other half keeps the physician alive.'" The reference to the physician here leads to one way that economics, politics, and ital food mix. Once all unnatural ingredients—additives and preservatives—are eliminated from the diets of the masses, someone's life is going to change. The people who cease to consume the additives will probably feel better and eat for less money, since they will no longer be paying for the production of the additive. And the people who produce the additives will be out of business. Some money and some power will change hands—shifting the scales to the benefit of the people. Moral justice will thus increase simply through ital food. As Rastas say, all things are overstood in fullness when looked upon with truth.

According to Hu-I, in order to overstand how to nourish the body properly, we must become familiar with its composition:

"Over 60 per cent water, the body contains many mineral elements in different amounts.

"Elements found in the normal body are hydrogen, phosphorous, chlorine, calcium, oxygen, carbon, magnesium, sodium, nitrogen, flourine, potassium, silicon, iron, iodine, and manganese.

"Cellulose is the framework of fruits and vegetables and supplies bulk, which aids in normal intestinal peristalis and stimulates the bowels.

"Fats supply energy in a very concentrated form and are fuel foods.

"Mineral matter supplies building materials and helps regulate the body processes. Mineral salts are necessary for blood making and tissue building.

"Proteins supply energy, and contain oxygen, hydrogen, nitrogen, sulfur, phosphorus, and a little iron.

"Water supplies building material and regulates the body's processes, making up the principal part of all the body fluids and secretions and helps make it possible for the body to regulate its own temperature."

All the fundamental elements the body needs, Hu-I says, are "bountifully supplied in natural foods, if not destroyed in their preparation. All life is furnished from within and must be replenished by living organic minerals in foods. Inorganic chemicals obtained from the drugstore are dead, and while they may stimulate for a time, they can give neither life nor health. Natural chemicals especially are needed for the purifying cleansing process: water, lemons, fresh pineapple, limes, peaches, grapefruit, oranges, tomatoes, and all juice fruit." Lack of certain minerals and elements is as easily identifiable as an overabundance, Hu-I explains:

"Potassium: Poor circulation and constipation denote a lack of potassium. Potassium foods should always be used in abundance in female troubles. All leafy vegetables, watercress, parsley, swiss chard, tomatoes, mustard greens, beetroot, spinach, and watermelon are sources of potassium.

"Sodium is very solvent. Abundance should be eaten in cases of rheumatism, hardening of the arteries, kidney stones, gallstones, stiff joints, acidosis, and diabetes. Spinach, okra, cucumbers, carrots, celery, beetroots, apples, and strawberries are sources of sodium.

"Organic iron is very important. It removes waste products and assists greatly in cleansing the blood stream. Inorganic iron should never be taken as it is an irritant to the kidney. Red and white cabbage, spinach, butt lettuce, raw carrots, cherries, strawberries, currants, and onion are sources of organic iron.

"Sulfur is especially needed in eliminating blood diseases, skin diseases, eruption, pimples, rheumatism. Foods containing sulfur aid in reducing: they stimulate the liver and promote the flow of bile. Cabbage, asparagus, raw celery, cauliflower, onions and radishes supply sulfur.

"Chlorine is a great destroyer of poisons. The presence of pyorrhea, Bright's disease, and gangrene always indicate insufficient chlorine. Chlorine foods also greatly assist in keeping the intestines clean. Raw white cabbage, spinach, radishes, fresh asparagus, parsnips, unpeeled cucumbers, raw carrots, watercress, lettuce, onions, and turnips are chlorine foods.

"Magnesium is nature's laxative. Foods containing magnesium are especially beneficial to persons suffering from autointoxication, constipation, and stiff and cracking joints. Apples, potatoes, barley, string beans, cabbage, coconuts, oatmeal, oranges, plums, brown rice, and watercress are rich in magnesium."

These elements, ailments, and remedies are simple aspects of Hu-I's detailed, fundamentalist medical perspective. Certainly, Rastafarians feel that the ital diet is the pathway to good health. For problems and diseases whose causes lie beyond the reach of ital food, thousands of herbal remedies can be concocted for cures. Ganja is included as a medicinal herb and is frequently brewed in tea and sometimes cooked in food for its beneficent, relaxing qualities. Ganja, of course, is also a divine herb, and Hu-I retreated to his confounding silence rather than further specify its curative powers. Rastafarians, as

This list is mimeographed and distributed to the bredren, sisters, and daughters of the Montego Bay Temple:

DENATURED FOOD   STAFF KILLED

OUR DIVINE THEOCRACY TEMPLE OF RASTAFARI SELASSIE I SAY THOU SHALT NOT EAT

Meat   *No alcoholic drink such as*
Fish   Rum
Salt   Beer
Eggs   Stout
Sardines   Wine
Bully beef   Brandy
Ham   Gin
Bacon
Chicken
Cheese
Patties   *No beverages such as*
                            Milk
                            Horlick
                            Ovaltine
                            Milo
No white flour product such as   Cocoa
Bread   Coffee
Buns   Soda
Cake
Dumpling
Gravy

extensions and manifestations of the Almighty, are obligated to exercise constraint and care over their physical health, as well as over their divine remedies. To do otherwise would be sinful.

Part of healthful living through ital food means abstinence from hard liquor, beer, wine, or spirits. If the Rastas had their way, the liquor empires of the world would entirely cease to exist. Rastas don't conceive of the sensation of drunkenness as a pleasurable one. Ganja, not alcohol, takes Rasta to the irie ites. "Reel and stagger like a drunkard" to a Rasta is one heavy put-down. The only liquid imbibed by Rastas which vaguely resembles alcohol is a brew called, simply, "roots." Rastas follow various recipes for making roots. It is homemade, probably through a process of fermenting the juices of some plants' roots.

The absence of alcohol and meat are two keys to the ital diet. The main key is somewhat ironic. A real, true Rasta will choose the ital diet, but he or she has no choice in the matter. If you are going to reach into life everliving, you must eat divinely, of life everliving. It's that simple.

11. SISTERS AND DAUGHTERS

No female member of Rastafari is referred to as a "mamma," "lady," "broad," or "chick." All females are called either "sisters" or "daughters," regardless of age, appearance, sexual, marital, or actual blood relationship. Both roles are accorded the natural familial connotations of respect, love, protection, and support. It is a goal of Rasta bredren that their sisters and daughters be relaxed, contented, at ease with themselves and their way of life —as Bob Marley would sing it, "No woman no cry."

Sisters and daughters learn through experience the rigors of childbearing and rearing, develop the skills of preparing ital food, and serve as positive female role models to the community. However, it is not unusual to find some bredren doing the cooking, or building fires, or performing other homemaking tasks while the sisters and daughters relax, play with the children, or talk among themselves.

In Deuteronomy 22:5 the Rastas find a clear statement of how men and women should dress:

> The woman shall not wear that which pertaineth unto a man, neither shall a man put on a woman's garment: for all that do so are an abomination unto the Lord thy God.

The Divine Theocratic Government of Rastafari follows this injunction explicitly, forbidding sisters and daughters to wear pants in any form. While the dress code is established, each sister or daughter at some point develops her own relative sense of propriety. Sisters and daughters are not permitted to enter a temple of Rastafari bareheaded and are rarely seen without their head wraps of colorful, printed cotton. The sisters and daughters would probably feel uncomfortable at times to have bredren gazing on their uncovered hair. This is prescribed in 1 Corinthians 11:5–6:

> But every woman that prayeth or prophesieth with her head uncovered dishonoureth her head: for that is even all one as if she were shaven. For if the woman be not covered, let her also be shorn: but if it be a shame for a woman to be shorn or shaven, let her be covered.

Sisters and daughters will be found in dress lengths varying from midcalf to floor, because it is thought that lust and crimes of passion and infidelity do not arise unless invited. A sister or daughter who shows her knees is inviting evil. Form-fitting, physique-revealing styles are not condoned, and within these restrictions, Rasta women seem to function with a serene sense of dignity.

They have a natural and balanced awareness of themselves, of beauty, and of grace. The practice of making up with cosmetics or adding any manner of unnatural enhancers to one's appearance is frowned on as devil's work and considered degrading to all the important, natural, and divine aspects of a person, male or female.

None of the sisters or daughters of Rastafari seemed to foster the jealousy, competition, or negative infighting which prevail among women in Western cultures, who have predominantly been socialized to believe that their worth lies in competing for and catching a man. Western women are raised to believe that to catch a man, they must develop the power of their beauty by investing millions of dollars in jars and bottles of vanishing, moisturizing, and firming creams, lotions and solutions, eye shadows, rouges, lipsticks, wigs, and figure flatterers. Rasta women don't feel that they'll have, or not have, a man because of the way they look. They rely on the fact that they'll have a man because of who they are, how they conduct themselves. The concept of cosmetic surgery, for example, is an abomination to the Rasta woman. A woman is what she is or isn't born with, and her worth in life is relative only to her acceptance of Rastafari, the resultant peace and love within herself, and her contribution to her family and community.

The sisters and daughters will listen but rarely offer more than a playful aside as the bredren sit around and "caucas" over the affairs of the world, Jamaica, and Rasta. If serious business is at hand, it is likely that women will not be. If serious ganja smoking is being done, it is rare for women to participate, although several women may partake of ganja together, behind the scenes.

This behavior may vary with the change of environment from rural to urban—the country sisters and daughters are more sheltered than those who participate in the daily street life of Kingston.

Many sisters and daughters are connected directly through specific men to the family of Rastafari, while others live outside Rasta camps and are free agents, espousing some, but not all, of the Rasta guidelines for dress and behavior. Some know the fundamental tenets of Rastafari, while others seem to simply accept that things are the way their man tells them they are. Because they come from Jamaica's roots, most are minimally educated: their schooling gets cut short by poverty and childbearing. Rastafari so far has not made the furthering of their education, and development of their awareness a serious objective.

The naturalist bases of Rastafarian world-view enjoin women from using birth control. Ras Hu-I warns:

"A woman start to hate the seed of a man by killing them . . . all sperm that go into a woman taking oral contraceptives will be dead. Where the dead have been buried? In the woman. So she become a sexpool of corruption. Panther [condom] put man into a sexmania. The man is a sexmaniac now, for him start to have sex by imagination, for it's not natural. So woman become the sexpool of corruption and man become the sexmaniac. That's what a society of intellectuals produces. Them na can't produce more than corruption."

While the Rasta moral code allows for sex between man and wife—usually joined by common law, but with community celebration and recognition—many sisters and daughters nonetheless become pregnant without a man to depend on. In most cases, the Rasta community comes to their assistance, to prevent their dependence upon Babylon in a time of need. This tends to prevent abortions, which the Rastas clearly consider to be mur- der, and it also keeps sisters and daughters out of the hands of the agents of Planned Parenthood, which dis- tributes birth control pills and other unnatural contracep- tive devices widely throughout the female roots of the Third World.

12.   HOLY GROUNATION

"Grounation" means the affirmation of life through the earth. It happens every year, the twenty-first of April, when the Rastas gather in a place in the countryside to commemorate the 1966 visit of Haile Selassie to Jamaica. Mortimer Planno, a leader from Kingston, happy to relax away from the tense violence of the streets of Trench Town, will solemnly tell you, exuding an unspoken pride, "Yes, sister, I did greet His Imperial Majesty, I did guide Him forth from the plane that brought him to this island. I offered him my hand to go down the plank, and he placed his in mine." That had been ten years before, and whether the Rastas today are an organized force or not, they have managed to coordinate ten successive grounations, with attendance growing, in the years that have passed, to confirm the fact that Haile Selassie lives in their minds and souls.

It may be the one time of year when poverty is not an obstacle, and is not allowed to interfere with plans. From all over the island, re-creating their 1966 pilgrimage to meet His Imperial Majesty, Rastas come—walking, riding, on motorcycles and in trucks and cars that defeat logic by continuing to run, heading for Castle Kelly, a hill which marks the approximate converging of the four parishes of St. Mary, St. Catherine, St. Ann, and Clarendon. No one knows exactly where Castle Kelly is, it's just a matter of getting close enough and sensing your way, or asking.

The journey began with our Rasta host, Hu-I, outside of Montego Bay, where his medical clinic is located. Members of his camp were busily preparing to leave, pouring rain water into large cans, fitting banana stalks, mangoes, and papaya into his car, rolling and storing their single changes of clothes. Hu-I appeared, resplendent in a cream-yellow safari suit like those worn by other brethren of his camp—pants legs trimmed vertically with handwoven stripes of the African colors, red, black, and green. Though unstated, his joy in the occasion was obvious and emanated from his relaxed figure, affecting everyone around him. After Bongo Lenny gave Hu-I's car a final under-the-hood inspection, Bongo Sewell, who functions as Hu-I's driver on these and other occasions, took the wheel, and we settled into the two cars to begin what we anticipated would be a five-hour journey. Hu-I's car was known for flying through the countryside, so it had already been agreed that they would keep watch for our car, driven by an American less certain of the twisting Jamaican roads and left-hand drive.

We followed Hu-I's "Rasta-mobile" out into the heat of the intense Jamaican sunshine, marveling at the visual image of the lead car: Pale yellow, with all manner of Rasta symbology and artistry identifying it and long dreadlocks streaming from the open windows as we left the tourist world of Montego Bay. Several miles beyond, we slowed to pass through an area where Jamaican men were laying badly needed new paving on the road. Glistening with perspiration from the heat and exertion, they stood alongside the road, leaning strained muscular bodies on their shovels and picks, smiling and greeting us, "Irie, bredren!" "Peace and love, Rasta," "Dread Rasta," "Praises due Selassie I." In the next town school children walking along the road shouted and waved as we flew toward Kingston. For the people do know Rasta, and, as Hu-I will tell you, they love Rasta. They admire his courage and strength, which uphold the highest convictions in the face of the same harsh poverty and oppression that they share on a daily basis.

The progress stopped just outside beautiful Fern Gully, where our car collided with a Jamaican-driven, road-hogging Buick. The pregnant Rasta daughter riding with us was all right, and we emerged from the car for the traditional roadside haranguing that accompanies the many accidents which happen on the island's poor roads. Hu-I, whose car stopped ahead, came directly back to me to ask quietly, searchingly, who was wrong. My answer given, he joined the bredren in a group which had formed to discuss the fault. As Americans, we would have been deemed wrong regardless of circumstance, except for the fact that we were in company with dread Rasta, whom no one wants to contradict too far. The

discussion concluded and we continued, with Bongo Sewell taking the wheel of our car and Hu-I driving his own. We stopped at a small hut where fruit is sold, to buy oranges and star apples to quench our thirst and replenish our energy.

Six hours out of Montego Bay, we were within reach of Castle Kelly and, after a few wrong turns, arrived at an area speckled with Rasta bredren and sisters wandering around, stretching their legs after their journeys. A pervasive atmosphere of peace and contentment was immediately evident, as long-time friends greeted and called out to one another. The cars parked, we unloaded and made our way up the large hill and down its slope among a small grove of trees with intermittent clearings, where Hu-I's people would camp for the three days of the grounation. Hundreds were already there, and from the hilltop I could see Rasta activity amid the bush— gathering wood, building fires, shredding coconut meat, stirring large pots of steaming rice and peas. Sleeping sites were constructed with overhead shelterings of canvas, roped from tree to tree. Framed photographs of His Imperial Majesty hung from branches, as did string sacks of oranges, blue BOAC bags, sheaves of bananas, articles of clothing. The men worked on converting the jungle into a home for themselves and their families, the women watched over babies, organized their provisions, and sat around talking and relaxing. A little boy, no more than two, ran to his mother, orange in hand, to ask for a knife. She nodded toward where his father was building their shelter, and the child went there to him. Smiling, the father handed him a knife half the length of his little arm, and the child deftly peeled the orange in the way Rastas do, removing the rind while leaving a covering to hold back the juice. He was natural and carefree with the large knife and returned it to his father so he could run off to play among his friends. Here the children are perfectly free—they can run and wander as they please, for it is known and accepted that, should they become frightened, anxious, or need anything, they can turn to anyone nearby and receive the same loving attention their own parents would offer. The extended family in action. It is simply, and beautifully, "overstood."

As the sun sank later in the day, camping preparations were concluded, and the newly created Rasta community moved up to the top of the hill, to form a congregation. Some of the daughters of Rastafari remained in their camp sites to watch over the babies and children who, full with the journey, excitement, and long hours of play, had fallen, exhausted, asleep. Everyone else migrated upward to the top of the hill, where they praised their own divinity in devotion to His Imperial Majesty Haile Selassie.

The bonfire burns huge and hot on the slope of the hill. At its crest, the hill boasts to the sky a circular palm-covered shelter. The smoke from the fire is thick but wafts incandescent as incense. The fire pops and crackles and small flecks of flame spark upward to the shelter in drifts of smoke.

The Niyabingi is heard here, raising the power of Earth to the sky. Through rhythmic beats on the heavy bass drum, you can feel the earth's very center—and the rhythms forming above the bass, from smaller drums, carry the Rasta cry of freedom and dignity into the sky above, lit with stars so bright they seem to point the way to eternity.

Here the bredren, the sons, the sisters and daughters of Rastafari have come to relax and share their innate power in nature. Some play the drums. Others dance in an unfrenzied, flowing motion. Each has his own, but all emanate from, and return to, the essential rhythm. Niyabingi.

Two young men, tall and lean, stand in subdued conversation, their dreadlocks casting shadows on their features so they appear as some holy apparition in the reflection of the firelight. The smoke drifts between them. This may be some reasoning on the nature of man. Or it may relate that the woman has come fruitful and will soon bear child. Or it may be that the kali grew high this year on the earth one cultivates. Whichever and whenever, it is free, You Are Free. A tall, dark Rasta, with red fabric fashioned to flow cape-like from his weary, young shoulders, stomps the outskirts of the fire, chanting, bringing the Masai from Africa to life in the Jamaican darkness.

The Niyabingi plays on into the night. And the night is deeper, darker, than has ever been seen. The Niyabingi is deep with the night.

The chanting in the circle plays in and out, through the toning of the drums. Each sings his own song, all sing the same song, "Carry Rastafari home." There is love, there is anguish, there is sorrow, there is pleasure, there is laughter and anger. Through everything, there is devotion, a certainty that this is a holy way of life, a certainty of manifesting divine principles.

The old woman,
weathered black skin taut against her bones of agony,
jumped the very earth,
screaming blood and desolation.
She of the veiled eyes
that ended nowhere, in their depth,
and the haunted body that housed no ghost,
no memory within,
she. Only the soul, that told her
her father's blood,
her son's blood,
the very energy that ran through
her family,
lay desecrated, wasted

seeping in to the ground's harsh thirst.
The drums beat on, the cadence rose,
the chant presumed to swallow reality itself.
And she jumped the very earth screaming
Blood, blood, blood.
My mother and my father, my blood,
my sisters and my children, my blood.
Feet down stomping,
she jarred her own
bones. The sound of them as thunder, iunder,
more dread by imagination, as it lingers,
a mind-echo.
She, jumping the very ground,
atrance with vengeance,
screaming blood for the
evil,
the pollution,
the desecration. Of her mother earth,
her blood.

13. THE ARTS: MARLEY'S MESSAGE

Bob Marley's music has the pulse of blood. It throbs, courses, beats, flies. It is always intoning content and purpose, filling the heart and draining it. Bob Marley is the king of reggae music. In Jamaica, the Caribbean, Africa, Britain, Canada, the United States, and elsewhere he has achieved superstardom. But if Bob Marley sees himself as a "star," it is in the Rasta sense and way of the word "star": shining, clustered beams of light and energy among the trillions that illuminate the harmony of a deep Jamaican night. Marley is not beyond staging *or* starring, but between his high-tension dreads, ganja, the music, and the vibes, the protective mantle and love of Rastafari exist and save him from all manner of "stage sickness."

The amount of ganja Bob Marley smokes could make an elephant dance! Ganja takes Marley up and over the rainbow of feelings, rhythms, and sensory modes that his music makes. And Rastafari is always with him, giving him spiritual authority and strength. Marley, in turn, lends Rastafari a contemporary expressive framework for reaching the roots. Singing that "everything that I do shall be upfull and right," Marley still sees himself as capable of the good and evil of man, but the positive qualities he aspires to in his music can be attained by anyone who seeks them. Marley himself attains them by singing

Rastafari, dancing Rastafari, sharing Rastafari, glorifying Rastafari.

Bob Marley has a message to deliver to his people, his roots. "New times, and if it's a new feeling, it's a new Zion. Oh, what a new day. Picking up? Are you picking up, now? Jah love, Jah love, protect us. Rastaman vibration, yeah, positive." Marley wants his song to reach blacks all over the world. He sings, "Play I on the r and b [rhythm and blues stations]. Want all my people a see. We're bubbling on the top one hundred, just like a mighty dread . . . Play I some music, this a reggae music." Whether by the grace of Rastafari, or because of a more progressive trend in the current popular music industry or a combination of the two, Bob Marley's music *is* being heard all over the world. Fifteen weeks after release, his latest album, *Kaya,* is bubblin' just over the top 100 (U.S.), which is no small accomplishment in a business where many recordings never even make it onto the charts. Marley is recognized as a top box-office draw, is high on the record charts in Britain, and has opened the road to success for other reggae artists like Boney M, whose single, "Rivers of Babylon," is riding the number one position on charts in Finland and Switzerland. Marley was recently awarded a Third World Peace Medal, presented by Senegal on behalf of all the African countries at the United Nations. Certainly no one has spread the message of Rastafari with greater reach or impact than has Bob Marley.

The pride of Rastafari is the driving wheel of Marley's music. And so, he is one among many Rastafarian artists. Painters, actors, dancers, sculptors, jewelers, and musicians follow the Rasta way of life all over Jamaica. Rastafari comes through their work visually and spiritually. Their creative capacities are at once amplified by the natural magnificence of their island and limited by its socioeconomic status. Very simply, for the Rasta woodcarver, the tourist market supplies the only reasonable income, yet the tourist market is both uninterested and unprepared for a full range of Rasta art. So, as in many other places and times, the Rasta artist in every trade faces the contradictory poles of true art and real survival. A deep commitment to Rastafari forces an even sharper sacrifice of the fruits of marketability, but then Rastafari provides a comfort, too. Even Bob Marley, at the superstar level, faces the pressures that are a part of Jamaica's neocolonial reality. While Jamaica can rarely provide him with sufficient electronic amplification to do his kind of concert, the roots want to know why he performs "foreign," out of Jamaica, more than he performs at home. So Bob Marley and all other Rasta artists encounter daily circumstances and situations which contravene their natural quests for unity, creation, and experience. They daily draw expressive strength, through the discipline and guidance of Rastafari, from these contraventions.

Marley, who grants the rare interview and often jests with the press, particularly outside of Jamaica, because the press is ignorant of the Rastafarian way of life, will demolish the superfluous question, as he did one afternoon while talking with Dermott Hussey of JBC Radio. Briefly speaking to questions about his split with the Wailers and other current happenings he found trivial, Marley said,

> "Music is music. You can tink of tings great and you can tink of tings simple. You know wha mean? Nobody know my idea of wha de Wailers supposed to be. People see images an ting and say das de Wailers. Right? Good. But music continues, ya know wha I mean. Me don see how you can jus play one music . . . Marley don't bow to superstitious tings. Me feel like I and I rule de earth, no cares which path run dis, no have no fears, not anywhere. Cas if sumting can corrupt you, you're corrupted already . . . Material tings . . . me don really understand plenty tings what people have to say . . . is so much tings people have to say. Every day I grow bigger. I mean, I and I grow, through experience. Me have seven children and me have to take care of dem. Simple ting about it is me talk about dem tings cause people ask me, but dat is not my trip, you know. My trip is to gather the children, you know you hear dem say gather de flock? Me no wan say it's a big ting, like is Moses or someting like dat. But me jus, all me do is beg Jah for give me work for do. Becau me useless if me don have noting to do. Me have to have sumting to do. So Him say, all right, I gon give you way for doing it, and I do it. So I'm free."

Only with Jamaica's transcendence of neocolonial status will every Rastafarian artist be able to join Marley in saying "I am free." They are all free within Rastafari, but then Rastafari is, and is not, of this world.

14.   TO AFRICA AND IRIE ITES

In many ways the Rasta world stands, in precept, spirit, and unity, against the world of Babylon, in a dialectic opposition. Whether this opposition will resolve itself through violence—the Babylon way—or through peace and love—the Rasta way—remains to be seen.

Rastafari is a revolutionary movement in the sense that it seeks freedom. Personal, individual freedom. Freedom of speech and expression. However, most revolutionary movements seek either internal or external change: the struggle is either to achieve freedom within oneself or to destroy oppression outside oneself. Rastafari seeks both courses.

Rastafarian priorities in Jamaica today are recognition, economic development leading to financial independence, an agri-based existence, political freedom, freedom of worship, freedom of movement, freedom of expression. Rastafarian revitalization of African styles of life and forms of art is a deliberate step which backs up the ultimate goal of physical emigration and settlement in Africa.

Some official governmental exploration into the possibility of transporting Jamaican nationals to Ethiopia to live occurred in the 1960s, but has not produced any concrete results. A Jamaican commission, composed of government, Rastafarian, university, and Ethiopian World Federation representatives, was appointed in 1960 to travel to Ethiopia and confer with officials there over the proposed Rastafarian immigration. While the commission found the heads of state of Ghana, Nigeria, Sierra Leone, and Ethiopia favorably disposed to accept skilled Africans from abroad into their nations, no formalizing steps have yet been taken, despite continuing correspondence between Jamaican officials and Rasta leaders to this end. It is also highly dubious that Jamaica's Rasta population in general has become more technically skilled over the past sixteen years.

The repatriation of blacks to Africa, from Jamaica or elsewhere, is, socially, economically, and politically, a potent and complex idea. It was once impossible for blacks in the Western Hemisphere to even think of visiting the continent of Africa. The primary roadblock was the negative self-image which denied African heritage, and the ultimate roadblock was financial. But today, thousands or more have made the voyage on vacations, on roots-finding missions, and to relocate permanently. It is this expansion of transcultural communication and experience that allows the commonalities of the diaspora blacks to actually be *seen* for the first time. Even if they cannot relate to African ways of life, American blacks —from Chicago, Houston, Los Angeles, New York, Boston, Atlanta, and elsewhere—have been able to visit Africa and become aware that there are black lands on this earth. Even as they have reached beyond the narrow boundaries of their own realities, blacks have not yet generated a ground swell to recreate an organizational effort to achieve the Back-to-Africa ideals that Marcus Garvey fathered in the 1920s.

And so it is with the Rastafarians. While perhaps more than half of Jamaica's population adheres, to some degree, to Rastafarian philosophy and lifestyle, there are no polls to show how many would actually repatriate to African lands, given the opportunity. However, as Rastafari continues to grow and spread among the youth—and future—of Jamaica, it will be precisely these kinds of choices that will accelerate the day of reckoning. Either Michael Manley will perform a veritable miracle in realigning the socioeconomic scales of the island so that the majority of Jamaicans have equal access to resources and opportunity, or the combined strength of the Rastas and the roots will "carry Rastafari home," as they say. Because the Rastas themselves are in a transitional phase, with the development and furtherance of their Divine Theocratic Government a major concern, it is difficult to predict their future. It is possible that they will continue to be a pervasive but loosely structured force in Jamaican life. But it is also possible that they will mobilize sufficient resources to approximate the organization now held by the Balailians (Nation of Islam) in America. Whatever the outcome, the future of the Divine Theocratic Government will depend to a great extent on how the Rastas exercise their political leverage with Jamaica's roots.

On the ideological plane, the Rastas have already exercised some leverage through the media of music, dance, theater, and literature. But it is the medium of reggae that has spoken the Rastafarian word most effectively and clearly to blacks in other lands. Reggae is the roots music of Jamaica even as soul is the roots music of black Americans. Both forms are capable of further transcending cultural differences, centering as they do on common themes of love, happiness, and eventual salvation, of "joy to the world." And the wave of the future—the fusion music which even now is blending the elements of soul, rock, blues, and jazz—opens the way for the Rastafarian message of peace and love to "cover the whole world, like a water cover the sea."

What would the world be like if Rasta philosophy rose and spread among most people? Ganja would be smoked practically universally: legalization would take place everywhere and quality and cultivation of herb would increase, with prices stabilizing because of an increase in its availability and opportunities for its production. Labor and industrial production would relate more directly to the fulfillment of human needs: things would be getting down to basics. No one, in other words, would be manufacturing, promoting, selling, buying, or creating sun reflectors, cosmetics, high-fashion items, additives, synthetics, contraceptives, pants for women, unisex clothing for anybody. The industrial energies which currently produce these things, along with alcohol, tobacco, and man-made drugs, would be refocused on housing, farming, ganja, artifacts used for the theatre and dance, herbal medicinal remedies, schools and educational apparatus, tools, and food. Language would be restructured, with new forms of expression, conception, and sound; and new combinations thereof arising.

African culture, values, and manifestations would supersede the Euro-Western orientation and probably would come to a meeting of the minds with many Eastern philosophies and cultures, which are predicated on some of the same basic principles. This would create a strong-based unification among more than two thirds of humanity and generate an atmosphere conducive to unprecedented cross-cultural communication. The Rasta, beyond his trenchant world view, is interested in all forms of humanity's positive expression and relates particularly well to those expressed through religion, art, and philosophy.

The Rasta world would be sparse, plentifully supplying necessities but underdeveloped in extraneous forms of technology and activity. In short, New Zion.

Human diversity and fulfillment in the experiential, educational sense would develop more from cross-cultural interaction than from manufactured forms of entertainment. People would spend their leisure hours making and listening to music, talking, smoking, dancing, acting, and meditating. The use of all forms of natural communication would expand. Most people would probably lose weight on the ital diet. Fat is a counterlife condition, in the Rasta view.

A new attitude toward life would arise. Which is what Rastafari is all about: *a way of life.*

APPENDIX: RASTA PROFILES

SISTER CHARLENE

Sister Charlene, a light-skinned young woman with pretty, round features and long, thick, waving brown hair, comes from a large, well-to-do family in Montego Bay. Her father has his own business; her sister has developed one which produces delightfully creative handmade dolls, puppets, and toys for children; and other members of her immediate family are professionally employed. Sister Charlene is educated and is one of the small number of Jamaicans with the option of "living the good life" on the island.

But Charlene has opted to live a comfortable but simple life with her husband, Paul. Their home contains a workroom, in which Charlene creates jewelry for her new enterprise, Abouti Designs, whose name she takes from an African tribe. "I think it's because I'm earth, by sign, that I like these kinds of things . . . they make natural sense. But of course it all depends on what your taste is, if you appreciate this kind of way."

The raw materials—stones, shells, paper, metal, wood, beads, cord, wire, and leather thong strips—are fashioned by Charlene into necklaces, earrings, and bracelets, to be sold in Montego Bay, Ocho Rios, and Kingston. Charlene says, "African styles are much more natural-looking and people are becoming more aware of the natural way of life, wearing more natural-looking things." Charlene's work doesn't stop with her jewelry— she also sews and is expert in the preparation of ital food, the mention of which sends a proud, glowing smile across Paul's face.

Charlene used to be a beautician but gave it up, she says, because it didn't suit her and she didn't find it satisfying. "I started finding myself when I saw, through Rastafari, what I was or what I am and what we mean of love. It gets lost all along the line of suppression."

Charlene and Paul are Rastas: photos and sayings of His Imperial Majesty Haile Selassie I hang on their walls, but they do not belong to a camp. They sometimes attend the services of the Ethiopian Orthodox Church, and neither of them is dread. "Lack," she says, is the vernacular for "no locks." "Dread and nondread is a matter of choice to the person . . . His Imperial Majesty is not dread, and he is a defender of the faith." Pants and skirts, she says, "are clothing only: I do not worship God by my clothing. I worship Him in other ways. There is no need for dogmatism—I can work in many ways." However, she feels that "we must have unity to demand respect as a group. We need unity in showing people the good and positive works that Rasta people do . . . when you hear 'Rasta' you always think of something dread and terrible."

Charlene talked with me about the problems of women within Rasta:

"I think men would appreciate it if women developed on a larger scale. I think they're conscious enough to accept this as being a good thing. But there are some who feel that the traditional role is needed. And I sometimes wonder for myself if you don't turn around and say that the woman should have been traditional, shouldn't have been liberated. Maybe the more time she spends with the children, the better.

"Unfortunately, the Rasta woman in the sect somehow has the role of housewife, mother . . . and due to poverty and having so many children, she's confined to that world. They probably can read and write, but only to a certain level. But then you also have Rasta women at a very educated level. I think the coming together of the two can make our freedom happen. We must teach the sisters and children as well."

RAS HU-I

In physical stature, Hu-I is small, wiry, and seems to be energy itself, even in the draining heat of Jamaican sun power. He wears a crown of long, thick dreadlocks that shadow his chiseled, planed face in the clear, bright, tropical light of day. This is the quintessential man, burning pure calories, wasting nothing, because he takes in nothing he has no use for.

Hu-I, native of Jamaica, went through medical educational preparation and became a doctor in England. He has since renounced all Western trappings and embraced Rastafari. The predominant manifestation of this fact is his medical clinic, which rests in a jungle-surrounded clearing west of Montego Bay.

The structure itself is geared to serve multiple purposes. A long low building with concrete walls, it is covered with a pieced, corrugated iron roof and its length extends from a tiny, one-room clapboard house painted brightly in green, red, and yellow. The clinic proper includes a waiting room, a laboratory of sorts unknown where Hu-I prepares his secret formulas for bottled herbal remedies, and various rooms in the rear where people may live until their illness abates—some stay, with Hu-I's sanction, because they have no where else to go or because they want to be there and Hu-I will guide them benevolently until they *do* go.

The visual impact of the outer walls of the clinic is powerful. Painted, a life-sized lion, blood dripping from his fangs, stands triumphant over a fallen and fatally wounded eagle. The image is accompanied by words:

Our Divine Theocracy Temple of Rastafari Selassie I Hath Prevailed. EAGLE, I ART TERRIBLE, and Dreadful is My Name, King of Kings and Lord of Lords, Selassie I. Eagle—America the great is falling.

No matter what the time, whether the clinic serves as a temple, meeting place, or haven from Babylon, there are people around. If there is no one there, it means that

Hu-I has gone from Montego Bay—to his farm in the hills or to points unknown.

The people arrive at Hu-I's with faith and truth showing through their expressions of pain and discomfort. They know that his power over the medicinal properties of herbs and plants is sufficient to cure whatever ails them. And Hu-I is loved, respected, venerated, not only among Rastas but by outsiders as well, for his proficiency in healing the sick and putting an end to pain and suffering. Hu-I himself says:

"My Father is the metaphysician. My Father doing that work again and give I. And because I was given as earth was created, I know all the medicinal ingredients that my Father put into plants and trees. In the time of need and worry, affliction and pain, I give my people healing from the tree because I know the different medicinal properties that they contain. And I know the various type of monsters that plague society, to which they cannot find a policeman to arrest those monsters. I can find you out the trees with the great power of Ras Tafari Selassie I. We know each other from the foundation. Jah. My people know I. Anywhere all over the world I go, my people find I because they know I, they follow I. Rasta is the only one that can give him comfort. No one else. They have leaders. They have wealth. But they have no comforter. And that's what love, co-operation, and unity are in a society, a comforter. I'm a comforter for my people. And because I am father, I am supposed to know when my people are sick or afflicted, and what I must do when there are certain diseases attack them. For is my children, that's my responsibility. Not Babylon responsibility, my responsibility. Or when you say it my father, you say it I. I'm in Selassie I, and Selassie I is in I. I do it. Nothing of myself but Ras Tafari who manifests his work through I. So I have great dominion and power, glory and authority. But I use my discretion. Not for myself. But I use it, like unto my Father, use it unto the oppressed nationalities. And my people love I, because I heal their afflictions."

BONGO LENNY

"Rastafari are people of upright quality. I and I manifest a spiritual accord. I and I, Rasta, was from Ethiopia, I and I come down here through colonialism, I and I come here to live a life of divinity to give people spirit that they could iturn to the land where they were found. I and I would have to project a liberty of the people, whosoever those people want to be. Outside of dat divine respect, them is not going to find it. Still I and I know dat dese people who instilled colonialism, dey are not going to give up easily. And I and I decide dat we must free from colonial links. I and I still don't come it gone. But even in dat divine manifestation, we will overthrow them, for de people will come with us.

"You would like to live forever? Den work in de behalf of Rasta. You must know what you're going to work for, whether to have money and to live a big life and die tomorrow, or work divinely through Rastafari and live forever."

BONGO SEWELL

"Live a royal life that others may admire you. Don't live the same level as your opponent and your adversaries.

They'll tromple you under brutal feet of might, for a host is a host and an individual cannot fight against his host. No individual. It takes the combined, the Trinity, some spiritual attainment, power—that's the only thing that can show you divine quality.

"The message of Rasta goes forward to other lands through telepathic inspiration. It comes from the Almighty Selassie I Rastafari.

"If every black man should seek and know dat dey are not from here and would seek to go home where dey come from, it would be better off.

"I gon show you de fullness of Rasta. What is written in de Bible, Rasta live above dat. Rasta principles are higher dan what is in de Bible. De Christians, Rasta live above dem."

RAS IYA GLENN

"Love yourself before you can love someone else. Criticize yourself before you criticize someone else. Develop yourself before you develop someone else.

"I and I wants to have bake shop, a food market, carpenter, plumbing. Rasta wants money for food. He can go without money for clothes and he will wear them and walk around tattered and look like a shipwreck and still be irie. Rasta don't care so much about shelter—he can pull up under a tree to sleep. Now, he need money to develop government. To have bus, tape recorder, radio.

"Where are you when you're between nowhere and the deep blue sea?"

BONGO SYLLY: IN THE LION'S DEN

The approach to Bongo Sylly's place is on the road to Ocho Rios. There, slatted, wicker-woven half-doors greet you: it says THE LION'S DEN, carved in wood. The structure houses Bongo Sylly and his work of wicker and bright fabric visuals, lions, and the Jungle. Outside, in the garden, the sun glances through the trees that bow gracefully overhead. Birds call their tropic distance from one another. All is irie. And Bongo Sylly is at work here, an artist in fullness. There are many visitors, and this busies the time.

Sylvester Ivery was born in Ewarton, a small town in the parish of St. Catherine, forty-six years ago. There were five brothers, two sisters, mother, and father in his family. Three of his brothers are also craftsmen. His father was a wickerworker and used to build chairs and things for a livelihood. The sons were never interested in his craft, but father Ivery gave them little chores to do and they learned to strip and weave the wicker. But the father eventually stopped working in his craft and began farming.

Bongo Sylly says that he was "going the wrong way in life" until he found Rasta. Some years after that, an important experience in his life occurred. He was working at the Silver Seas hotel, a large luxury complex on the North Shore, just west of Ocho Rios. Mr. Sharpe, an owner of the hotel and Bongo Sylly's benefactor and boss, was in the hotel, and Bongo Sylly was out at the pool, where he worked. At the time, Bongo Sylly was dread, and the guests used to come out to the pool and ask him questions. He heard Mr. Sharpe call to him, telling him not to come out of the work shed. He later learned that the police had been to the hotel in connection with the fact that a veritable war was going on between Babylon and Rasta in Montego Bay. Mr. Sharpe had told the police that Bongo Sylly was "his," and so they left. Mr. Sharpe put Sylly into a taxi, to go home to safety, but the police followed him, stopped the taxi, and made Sylly get out. Though they let him go, the next Monday morning they caught him again, arrested him and, as Sylly described it, "troubled me in prison. They put me in prison and cut me locks. And it's eight years since then I grow my locks and not use razor."

Today, Sylly says,

"They no trouble me so much with herb. I never intend to do business with herb. I intend to use herb to cleanse the mind. Herb can set people mad because people build a fear of it; they don't know how to accept it and use it. If I have anything to do that's evil, the herb will wash it out."

Sylly continues to talk about the things that are on his mind. Even though he's mad at the government because they won't run a water pipeline up to his place but have put one in for his Chinese neighbor, he says,

"This is the first government that deals with Rasta at all. People in the past have just known that Rastafari was just like a wild animal . . . Rasta comply with Manley and assist him against crime and violence. Many bredren would be better off without this way of life, of crime and violence. Thousands of people lose their lives in Kingston. The people don't give thanks to Manley, but he keeps them from being slain by [former Prime Minister Hugh]

Shearer. Jamaican people loved [former Prime Minister] Bustamante—he gave them cheap clothes, cheap food, and they like it. I was here when the most important clothes in Jamaica was khaki suit, or something made from a burlap bag. But I see somewhat these clothes again as history repeats itself."

A small plane flew over the garden very low, blowing up dust. Sylly continued: "Jamaica's changing, so we wanna build out the people differently, away from so much wickedness. Bongo Sylly believe in Jamaica, but him tired of working for Jamaica with no pay."

And the work Bongo Sylly does for Jamaica you can see in his little jungle, or "research," as he calls it. He uses wicker that he brings back from a secret place in the deep hills—white hook, red silver jack, and bastard palm heart. He boils them, dries them, strips them. Bongo Sylly also uses mahogany and other hardwoods for carvings and must go with a truck to St. Mary or St. Ann to get this wood.

The entire structure is of wicker, bound and woven into arched doorways, with planting stands aligned to the sides. A bar-type structure, totally front-faced of wicker, with a giant, blown-glass bottle, also covered in wicker, is centered in the room. Graceful arches, loops, and curves form areas in the open space of the structure. Two lions face each other above the planters as you enter another room. They are carved of wood and stained dark at the mane, claws, and tips of tails.

Bongo Sylly gets very peaceful in his "research," one of which he built many years ago, as a creative approach to tourism. He built the research because he feels that foreigners who visit should be able to have a place where they can walk among all the beautiful varieties of plant life generic to the island, taste all of its native fruits and vegetables, hear its music, see its different forms of art and craftwork. This way, Sylly says, people come to achieve a more total picture of a place as they travel through it, and strangers can learn to appreciate one another as they experience Jamaican culture together.

Sylly's jungle remains peaceful until someone treads against Rastafari or performs some unjust or negative action. Then Bongo Sylly will become agitated, starting to mutter, "It make me mad, it make me mad." Many Jamaicans, including Rastas, live on the island without being able to fully appreciate its beauty and diversity. Sylly does appreciate Jamaica, but he is anxious for it to reach its potential. Bongo Sylly becomes frustrated by things that work against that achievement.

NYAN'S STORY

Nyan says it was no ordinary event that led him to Ras Tafari:

"Christ promised and say, the things that I did in this time, when your time come, which *is* this time, the things that I and I shall do will be even greater. He promised that. Him say he shall send the comforter unto you and shall teach you all things. So I and I, Rastaman, a spiritual man. I tell I and I, no, I don't believe until I see. I can show you.

"I was at home that whole day. That was in 1963. And I had reasoned with my father the whole day after I sent the children out to school. And in the evening when the children come home and I give them them dinner, I tell them to drive in the goats, we have some goats and them sleep underneath in the cellar. Well, it have a door, and de door hinges up here and de door lock down dere, and lock on a big four-by-four post. And my little daughter, Marla, was five years old at the time. She had to help me drive in the goats. And she was lowering the door down to the bottom part, and the billy [goat] jump in and bounce the stick dat was holding it. And de door drop right down upon her finger, down dere now. Seen? And the powers within I tell I say man, I get hurt, you know, and I go and I jump up and go out and dese two fingers dem taken off, because you see it's a big door to em pretty little finger, and deep down I say, I know it. The hospital, that's what was flashing in on my mind, run to hospital. And as clearly I speak to you, the power, the next man, the higher man, him say, niyaman, I and I is here from morning, you know all things are possible unto I-man, and man no think of hospital. And dere and den I just feel dat pressure drive in me, and I just slam myself down on my knee. And I just kept Marla's hand so, and I didn't say eight words. Then I say, Marla, see your finger there. That vibration, the power now, dat take I man, dat sweat de whole shirt, pants, everything just wet, you know? I have to wait and pray and wait and pray, 'til dat emotion pass. When I done, about thirty minutes after I'm going through dat. An when I finish I call her forward again, and I confess to my Father, 'Well, Father, what I really want was her dear little finger again.' I say 'Marla, come, let me see your finger.' 'See it, dada. No blemish!' Seen? So I just know."

RASTA MAN (ODE TO THE RASTAFARIAN*)

& On to be a Rasta Man
Shore & gone
Up in de hills
I's stretched Out
Before the choke & cough
Of Kingston towne.

O to be a Rasta Man
Burnin to the brim
In majesty
As Ethiopia
Bronze god of timeless aegis
Axum pillars
Back to the East
A time of peace.

Natty Natty
Dread
     Jah
The rushing red

Of regal veins
BLOOD
Is a Rasta
Turned on to himSelf.

O Marcus
Marcus Garvey
Mark us dark
With Africa
& tell us:
Is we prophets
Here to bleed
Us wounds here to heal?

Down from Asmara
Up on Negrito
Comes these fierce suns
Of the Western horizon.
Rise on/Rise on

Rasta! Rasta!
Om Rasta!
Teach us with
the oak of your feathered touch
The calm gait of your gaze;
Show us grass-keyed
Portals of forgotten streams,
Not to flee
Or Plea
To gods
or Masters
No

Show us the view
From mountaintops
Of mornings
Robed with the smell of cocoa
nut dew
Do it again

Rasta Man
Like the soothing balm
Of red sun-setting
On skin-black Night
Blending In
To myth-times of
Mothers & Fathers
Stark before the alter
Deep & down within.

Sweet brotha Rasta Man
As burnin Weed
Pearls from your eyes
Race the eons
For our children
To know
Where we were
& Where we go:
  —Khadjuka (Don Mizell)

NOTES

Chapter 1

1. Orlando Patterson, "Slavery and Slave Revolts: A Sociohistorical Analysis of the First Maroon War, 1665–1740," in Richard Price, ed., *Maroon Societies* (Garden City, N.Y.: Anchor Press/Doubleday, 1973), p. 249.
2. Janheinz Jahn, *Muntu: An Outline of the New African Culture,* trans. M. Grene (New York: Grove Press, 1961), p. 51.

Chapter 2

1. From "The Ghost (Marcus Garvey)," on *Garvey's Ghost,* Mango Records LTD., 1975, written by Burning Spear, published by Island Music (BMI).
2. Marcus Garvey, *The Philosophy and Opinions of Marcus Garvey,* ed. Amy Jacques-Garvey (1924–26; reprinted New York: Arno Press/New York Times, 1969), p. 125.
3. Ibid., p. 34.
4. Ibid., p. 412.
5. Ibid., p. 44.
6. Ibid., p. 324.
7. Ibid., p. 9.

Chapter 3

1. Kwame Nkrumah, *Neo-Colonialism: The Last Stage of Imperialism* (New York: International Publishers, 1956), pp. ix, xi.

Chapter 5

1. John Hearne and Rex Nettleford, "Our Heritage," Department of Extra-Mural Studies, University of the West Indies (Kingston, Jamaica: Herald Ltd., 1963), p. 18.
2. Loc. cit.
3. Haile Selassie, Eighteenth Anniversary Address, delivered November 2, 1948, Addis Ababa, Ethiopia.
4. *Jamaica Daily Gleaner,* April 21, 1966, p. 1.
5. Ibid., April 22, 1966, p. 1.
6. Haile Selassie, Address, delivered at Stanford University, Stanford, Cal., 1964.

Chapter 7

1. J. Cogswell, *Hebrew Theocracy: A Treatise* (New Brunswick, N.J.: Press of J. Terhune, 1848), p. 6.

PREFACE

Shortly after arriving in Jamaica, for the second time in eight months, I met with Ras Mortimer Planno and two other Rastafarians. It was a scorchingly hot day in Kingston. We drove to a small street in Trench Town and arrived in front of the only painted building on the block. The colors on the building were the vivid Rasta colors signaling their organization. Entering the cool interior of the building was a relief—but only temporarily. The nine Rastas awaiting us there were quiet and stony-faced, with as many styles of dreadlocks as there were individuals. In the sparsely furnished room, they formed a circle, seating me in the middle. Mortimer Planno and I had previously spent many months in intensive discussion and debate over the concepts that he was now about to present to the Rasta Council. After a general greeting to his brethren, Planno began to painstakingly read from the proposal for this book. During the two hours that followed, I did not speak nor did anyone address me. Only an occasional, recognizable response from the assemblage came through: "CIA agent!" . . . "Fire unto the man!" . . . "Agent from Babylon!" I was sweating. Since it was an open meeting, any new Rasta entering at any undetermined time had to be given a recapitulation of the proposal for this book. The time dragged, and finally, still not having spoken, I was returned to my hotel.

On the following day, as the sun reached its apex, I returned to the Rasta High Council. I had made mental note to those who were in doubt, and it was to them that I addressed my speech when I was finally allowed to speak. Their main concern centered around the unfavorable coverage that depicted them as "rude boys" and "criminals." As I spoke, a man who had been silent for the entire two days began to be loudly and overtly abusive to my presentation. He was asked to leave by the others, and when he did not comply he had to be physically subdued. They decided, on the basis of his actions, that he was not a "true" Rasta, but perhaps a local *agent provocateur* who would have used the gun he carried to further distort their image. The seriousness of their concerns and of my position became evident.

A young newcomer to the proceedings challenged me and I provided him with with a parable: "Look upon me like a vehicle—a car. A car will not go anywhere unless you drive it. I come to you like a car—driverless. I make myself available to you to be driven. I cannot drive myself. I am in your control, to be driven as you see fit, to see what you wish me to see."

Kingston was one beginning. Each new photo was a

new beginning. Whether it was in Ocho Rios, Negril, Montego Bay, or elsewhere in Jamaica, the scene I have just described took place, repeatedly, before I was ever allowed to take the first photograph for this book. Each photo produced its own interpersonal encounter. Not one contact automatically opened the door to another. My last hurdle was to introduce the writer—a woman. A Rasta society is a male-oriented society. Ras Planno had warned me to wait until I was accepted before introducing the concept of a woman writer.

My difficulties in taking these photos are a testimony to my reason for wanting to make this pictorial journey, *Rastafari: A Way of Life*. Embodied in the previously described incident, and the subsequent ones are all the myths that we entertained about one another. To dispel myths is no easy task.

The purpose of this book is to bridge the gap between the reality and the mystique of the True Rastafarian. To accomplish this I had to come to grips with the myopic images to which I had been subjected. I had to try to avoid the traps of the tourist-version Rastafari, which was easily accessible. In wanting to produce an alternative to the sensationalized view of the Rastas, I had to cut through and untangle the undergrowth of reality and fiction. In doing this I began to understand and visually produce a singularly different dimension in Rastafari. I hope that the unifying singularity is the *human* dimension. I feel confident and successful about having presented an alternative image. I will feel completely successful if the Rastafarians I shared time and space with feel that this is a fair and representative picture.

I was fortunate enough to share this project with a sensitive writer, Tracy Nicholas, and with my editor, Marie Dutton Brown, who believed and shared my enthusiasm.

Seen.

Bill Sparrow
1977

Seen!

Ras Hu-I: "To grow dreadlocks, you just wash it and leave it, that is all."

Irie.

A Rasta child is born into a Rasta family, but will live forever in the family of I
and I.

Bongo Lenny: "Rastafari still don come, it's gone."

I and I look onto the world, a child of dread.

Peace, love, and praises make smiles.

:

In sunlit innocence, all Jah's children are friends.

The material plane for many Rastas is a bare and simple one. It is in the heart, the mind, the spirit of Rastafari that they live in wealth and abundance.

As I and I reason with my Father, I and I come to know truth.

Of the land and for the land . . .

Ras Hu-I: "Love, Purity, and Holiness shall cover over the earth like a water cover the sea."

Ras Hu-I: "In the time of need and worry, affliction and pain, I give my people healing."

Even in youth: assurance, security . . .

Ras Hu-I: "My people love I . . . They follow after I."

Bongo Sewell, Saint-I: "I and I are a sheep-like people."

Bongo Lenny—Love, Devotion, and Surrender.

Niyabingi.

Chant praising Rastafari Selassie I.

"Children of I and I will know to speak the language spoken in Zion, what the people call heaven. They will know to speak Amharic."

Ras McLean: "In the core of Rastafari, I and I live forever, a divine inspiration growing."

Ras McLean: "As a son of Rastafari, I and I carry love and color, this art, in the shanties of Trench Town."

I and I go beyond politics for a spiritual diagnosis.

"Music and art are life: no pain, no sickness, no woe. My pride shines only from the pride of Rastafari Selassie I."

Ras Mortimer Planno with painting "Firegate" in Kingston. On the painting is written: "EAGLE, I ART TERRIBLE, and Dreadful is My Name, King of Kings and Lord of Lords, Selassie I. Eagle—America the great is falling."

His Imperial Majesty Emperor Haile Selassie I: in art, in life, in light, the center of Rastafri.

Ras Coghill Leghorn, actor and artist.

All art, all visions, all life, come from the word of Jah.

Ras Dubrick Edwards, acclaimed painter, Kingston.

Ras Dubrick, the Bible, palm fronds, and his vision of Revelation: "And one of the elders saith unto me, 'Weep not: behold, the Lion of the tribe of Judah, the Root of David, hath prevailed to open the book, and to loose the seven seals thereof" (5:5).

"Self-portrait," by Ras Dubrick.

Sister Charlene Blake: "I started finding myself when I saw through Rastafari what I was and what I am and what we mean of love."

Rastas seek the alternative lifestyle: even in poverty they work for themselves and Rastafari.

Glendevon, in back of Montego Bay.

"Here the children are perfectly free."

"Everything shall be upfull and right."

"For the hurt of the daughter of my people am I hurt; I am black . . ." (Jeremiah 8:21).

"Jah, Rastafari, carry Rastafari home . . ."

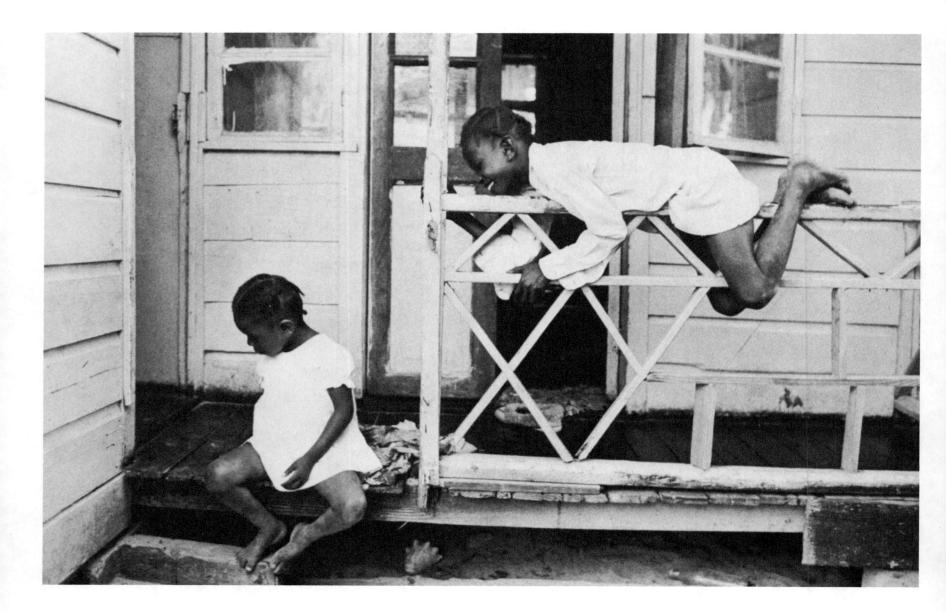

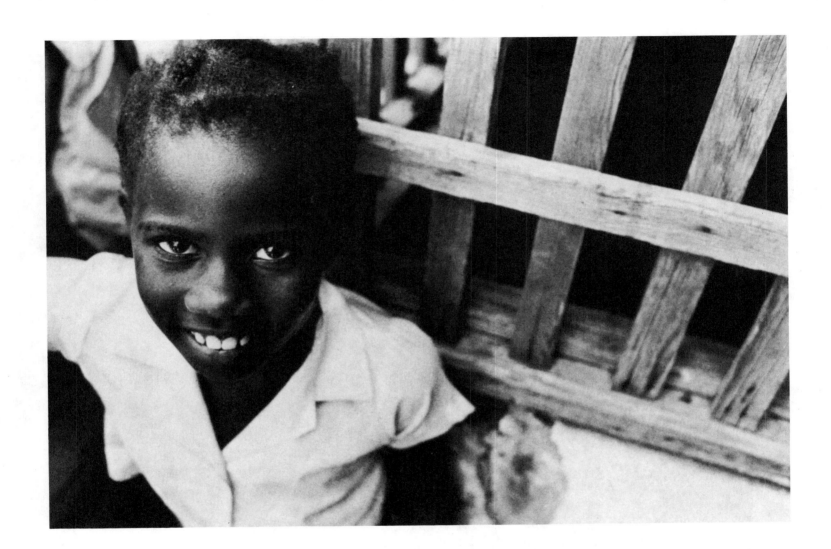

"Gon make me tam, wan for shelter me dreads from Babylon."

"Wordsound is power. Just the chant of Iya Glenn is the Inspiration to take me higher."

"No woman no cry."

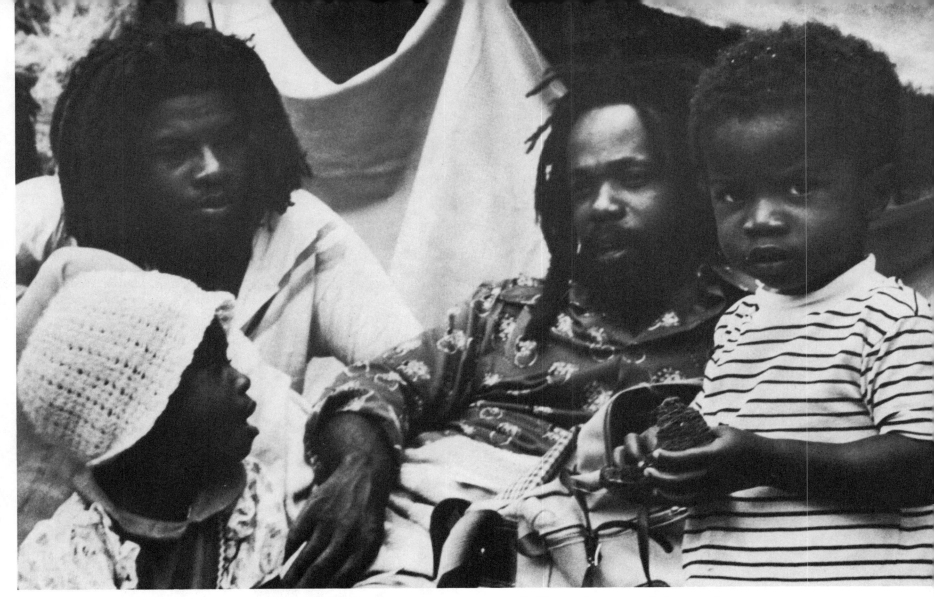

Bongo Lenny at Holy Grounation: "You would like to live forever? Den, work in de behalf of Rasta. You must know what you're going to work for, whether to have money and to live a big life and die tomorrow, or work divinely through Rastafari and live forever."

Lighting the *chillum* pipe.

Ganja, the mystic herb.

In nature from nature, divine illumination.

Grating coconut. It replaces meat in the flavoring of ital food.

Bongo Congo Bongo I.